A2 Law

UNIT 6

AQA

Module 6: Concepts of Law

Peter Darwent & Jennifer Currer

Philip Allan Updates
Market Place
Deddington
Oxfordshire
OX15 0SE

Tel: 01869 338652
Fax: 01869 337590
e-mail: sales@philipallan.co.uk
www.philipallan.co.uk

© Philip Allan Updates 2005

ISBN-13: 978-1-84489-003-3
ISBN-10: 1-84489-003-1

This guide has been written specifically to support students preparing for the AQA A2 Law Unit 6 examination. The content has been neither approved nor endorsed by AQA and remains the sole responsibility of the authors.

Printed by MPG Books, Bodmin

Environmental information
The paper on which this title is printed is sourced from managed, sustainable forests.

Contents

Introduction

■ ■ ■

Content Guidance

■ ■ ■

Questions and Answers

Introduction

About this guide

The AQA specification for the AS and A2 Law examinations is divided into six modules. The guide for Unit 6, **Concepts of Law**, is very different from the guides for Units 1–5. While it does contain specific material on the concepts of Law and morals, Law and justice, Balancing conflicting interests, Fault and Judicial creativity, it is essential that you are aware from the outset that in order to demonstrate knowledge and under-standing of these particular topics, you must utilise appropriate knowledge of legal processes, institutions and substantive law, gained in the study of the other modules.

For example, when addressing the issue of fault as the basis of criminal liability, it is necessary to consider *mens rea* as the principal element in determining the blame-worthiness of the offender, the requirement that the *actus reus* is voluntary and the various defences which eliminate or reduce fault. Other relevant areas, depending on the nature of the question, are those of strict liability and the tort of negligence.

When considering the subject of judicial creativity, you need to be able to discuss the doctrines of precedent and statutory interpretation and proceed from these to consider how and why judges in this country do not merely give decisions in cases before them but actually make new law, or at least develop and extend existing legal rules.

In discussing how law acts to balance conflicting interests, consideration of contract law, especially consumer protection rules, or of nuisance will be particularly useful to demonstrate knowledge of this topic.

The concept of justice can be illustrated by any number of references to previously learned material, such as provision of legal aid, independence and impartiality of judges, use of jury trials, and burden and standard of proof in criminal and civil cases.

The theme of law and morality can be examined within the context of serious criminal offences, which clearly flout basic and traditional conventions of morality, e.g. 'Thou shalt not kill' is an accepted moral rule reflected in the UK's homicide laws.

The examples referred to above are by no means exhaustive, but are indicative of the illustrative material that may be used.

Within this unit, you are also required to criticise and evaluate existing legal rules and to consider them in wider contexts — social, ethical and political. On occasions, you will have the opportunity to express your own opinions and ideas, provided they are well supported and clearly explained.

There are three sections to this guide:
- **Introduction** — this provides advice on how the guide should be used, an expla-nation of the skills required to complete the unit successfully and guidance on revision and examination techniques.

- **Content Guidance** — this sets out the specification content for Unit 6. It also contains references to materials drawn from units studied previously, to enable students to demonstrate a fuller understanding of each Unit 6 topic.
- **Questions and Answers** — this section provides sample answers to typical examination questions on each topic area. Each question has an A- and C-grade answer. Examiner comments show how marks are awarded or why they are withheld.

How to use this guide

The Content Guidance section covers all the elements of the Unit 6 specification, breaking each topic down into manageable sections for initial study and later revision. Given the nature of this unit, it must be stressed that this section is not intended to be a comprehensive and detailed set of notes — the material needs to be supplemented by further reading from textbooks, and illustrative material needs to be augmented by considering relevant examples from materials previously studied. Students are also strongly encouraged to read quality newspapers on a regular basis, and to use relevant legal websites and law journals, especially *New Law Journal* and student 'update' magazines.

Learning strategies

It is essential to build up a good set of notes for successful A2 study, and this is particularly important for this unit. Ideally, you should compile a set of notes by drawing on a number of sources: classroom teaching, this guide, other textbooks and, as recommended above, quality newspapers and legal journals. These notes need to include:

- accurate definitions with brief explanations
- the key cases to be used for each topic

Revision planning

At this level of study, it is essential that you understand the need to learn factual information thoroughly. Do this as the module is being taught. Don't leave it to the revision stage, otherwise you will find there is simply too much detailed information to absorb. Remember that skimming over some notes or reading this guide is not revision if you have not already learned the material.

The first stage of revision requires organisation of all your work. You should ensure that:

- your class notes are up to date
- you have understood the main points of each topic in this guide
- you have made accurate notes on any wider reading
- you have made clear notes about case studies, stating both the key facts and, more importantly, the legal reasoning behind decisions

The next stage is to summarise all of the material, organising it under the headings and subheadings of the Unit 6 specification. During the revision period, you should go over all your notes and reduce them to manageable proportions. This is, in itself, an effective learning exercise. The act of summarising makes it easier to recall the material and should reduce the chance of forgetting parts of it in the examination. The greatest number of exam marks are not lost through failure to understand the material, but simply through forgetting fuller explanations.

Assessment objectives

Assessment objectives (AOs) are common to AS and A2 units and are intended to assess a candidate's ability to:

- recall, select, deploy and develop knowledge and understanding of legal principles accurately, and by means of examples
- analyse legal material, issues and situations, and evaluate and apply the appropriate legal rules and principles
- present a logical and coherent argument and communicate relevant material in a clear and effective manner, using correct legal terminology

Examination technique

First of all, familiarise yourself with the style of questions for this particular unit. Learn from these questions and the AQA mark scheme what the Potential Content is for each question, and how marks are allocated across the different mark bands. The last section of this guide — Questions and Answers — is designed to provide guidance about the techniques required for this unit.

Case studies

The importance of case references cannot be overemphasised and without these it is impossible to demonstrate a sound understanding of relevant law. A 'case-free' answer rarely obtains more than a D or E grade, and will more often be awarded a U grade. The mark scheme also often prevents examiners from awarding marks if there is no reference to case or statutory authorities. While the facts of cases are certainly relevant, the most important aspect of case law is the issue of the legal reasoning employed by senior judges in order to arrive at their decision. Learn to state briefly the basic facts of the case and then go on to explain fully the legal reasons behind the actual case decision. Study the way in which key cases are used to demonstrate a fuller understanding of a topic, or to illustrate a key issue or argument, in the Questions and Answers section of this guide.

QWC marks

Ten marks are awarded on each A2 paper for the quality of written communication (QWC). The easiest way to lose some of these is to misspell basic legal words such as *grievous*, *defendant*, *deterrence*, *assault*, *precedent*, *sentence*. Check your spelling, use paragraphs correctly and make your handwriting as clear as possible.

Planning your answers

When you look at the A-grade answers in the Questions and Answers section of this guide, you will recognise that they have a clear structure, usually demonstrated straight away by a simple, accurate and relevant first sentence. The opening section immediately addresses a key element of the question set, relevant topics are clearly identified with sound explanations provided, and there are many case references that underpin the explanation or argument. Finally, there will be a short paragraph which both summarises the major points of law already explained and provides a clear conclusion. C-grade answers lack this element of planning and structure.

You should read the exam question carefully, make sure you understand what it is asking and then make a short plan — it could be in the form of a spider diagram or just a series of headings and subheadings. After this, read the question again to check that your plan is both relevant and accurate. Don't worry about crafting a lengthy introduction to your answers — look carefully at how the A-grade answers start and model your own technique on these.

Time planning

Contrary to popular belief, few students have a problem with lack of time in the examination. By doing homework essays and timed or practice examination essays you will learn whether you are a quick or a slow writer. If you feel that you are likely to have a time problem, planning your response is even more vital. You will have to learn how to write full answers in no more than 35–40 minutes. Remember this examination is 90 minutes — 15 minutes more than the time set for Units 4 and 5.

Those who finish early — and this will apply to most candidates — should first check their answers to ensure that they have included key legal rules and appropriate cases. Next they should look at their plans to ensure that they have covered all the points. If at the end of this process there is still time left, they should consider what additional material can quickly be added, such as a further case.

Content
Guidance

The specification for Unit 6 outlined in this section covers the following topics:

Law and morals
- Characteristics of legal rules
- Characteristics of moral rules
- Distinctions between legal and moral rules
- The relationship between legal and moral rules
- Coincidence of legal and moral rules
- Divergence of legal and moral rules
- Natural law theorists
- Positivists
- The Hart–Fuller debate
- The Hart–Devlin debate

Law and justice
- The meaning of 'justice'
- Theories of justice
- The extent to which substantive legal rules, legal institutions and procedures achieve justice

Balancing conflicting interests
- Theorists
- Balancing of conflicting interests by Parliament
- Balancing of conflicting interests by the courts
- Balancing conflicting interests in criminal law
- Balancing conflicting interests in the law of tort

Fault
- The meaning of 'fault'
- Fault in criminal law
- Fault in the law of tort
- Fault in the law of contract
- The importance of fault

Judicial creativity
- Characteristics of the doctrine of precedent which limit judicial creativity
- Characteristics of the doctrine of precedent which aid creativity
- The extent to which judges are able to display creativity in statutory interpretation
- The balance between the roles of Parliament and the judiciary
- Policy
- Should judges create law?
- Judicial preference

Law and morals

Characteristics of legal rules

Sir John Salmond, writing in the early twentieth century, described law as 'the body of principles recognised and applied by the state in the administration of justice'. John Austin, in his book *The Province of Jurisprudence*, defined it as a command issued from a sovereign power to an inferior and enforced by coercion. In Britain this sovereign power is Parliament, although legal rules are also made by judges.

Compliance with legal rules is compulsory, not a matter of choice. They are imposed on and govern all members of society and must be obeyed. In Britain everyone is bound by the **Offences Against the Persons Act 1861**, which stipulates (among other things) that people cannot intentionally or recklessly cause serious harm to another. The same principle applies to judicial decisions, for example *R* v *R* (1991), which established that a man could be found guilty of raping his wife.

Breach of legal rules will result in state sanctions and procedures. For example, breach of the criminal law may result in being arrested, charged and prosecuted through the criminal courts. If a person is found guilty, a criminal sanction, such as a fine or a period of detention, may be imposed. With reference to the **Offences Against the Persons Act 1861**, for example, breach of s.20 may result in a maximum sentence of 5 years' imprisonment.

Legal rules are made and take effect at a precise time. A precedent is created in the judgement of a case and applies to future cases in lower courts. A piece of legislation will take effect on a specified commencement date.

> **Tip**
>
> Examples of laws from virtually any part of the specification can be cited here.

Characteristics of moral rules

Phil Harris, in *An Introduction to Law*, defines a society's 'code of morality' as a set of beliefs, values, principles and standards of behaviour.

Compliance with moral rules is voluntary in that people have a choice as to whether or not they obey them. People make personal decisions as to what they consider to be moral and immoral, and they may or may not be persuaded by the validity of a moral rule. It follows that the moral duties of different individuals will vary. What one person considers immoral, another may not. For example, some people may believe that sex before marriage is immoral, while others consider it to be acceptable.

Moral rules develop gradually. They often stem from religious rules made thousands of years ago. Over time, conduct once considered immoral increasingly becomes acceptable. For example, the attitude towards homosexuality continues to change.

Moral rules are enforced informally, usually through social or domestic pressure. A person who repeatedly tells lies or breaks promises, for example, may be shunned or ostracised by friends, family or work colleagues.

Distinctions between legal and moral rules

Many of the distinctions between legal and moral rules emerge through a discussion of their characteristics. It is useful, however, to consider the following distinctions:

- If there is disagreement regarding the content of a legal rule, then reference can be made to a precedent or Act of Parliament to resolve the disagreement. Whether or not people agree with the legal rule, they will be able to accept what it constitutes. This cannot be done with moral rules, which are not scientific proofs and are open to dispute.
- Legal rules can be changed instantly whereas moral rules gradually evolve. The legal rules regarding homosexuality were instantly changed when the **Sexual Offences Act 1967** was passed. Society's moral acceptance of homosexuality, however, underwent and continues to undergo gradual change.
- Another distinction is that of enforcement. Legal rules are formally enforced by state sanctions and procedures. Moral rules are informally enforced through social and domestic pressure, and are often supported not by threats of punishment, but by a simple reminder of the rules' existence, and by an implied appeal to act in accordance with them.
- Legal rules can impose strict liability. This can be seen in both criminal and civil law. The **Trade Descriptions Act 1968** aims at protecting consumers by outlining strict liability offences. In civil law, the tort of nuisance is concerned with preventing interference with the enjoyment of proprietary interests. Moral offences, however, can only be committed voluntarily with full *mens rea*.

When we identify the distinctions between legal and moral rules it is important to consider also the pluralistic nature of society. The moral codes of the various groups making up British society may vary, but all are obliged to comply with legal rules.

The relationship between legal and moral rules

Any legal system presupposes a certain amount of morality, because if law is not essentially moral there is no easy explanation of the obligation to obey. The relationship between law and morality can perhaps best be described as two intersecting circles, with the area inside the intersection representing the common ground between the two spheres, and the areas outside representing the distinctive areas in which each holds exclusive sway.

> **Tip**
>
> Candidates are required to explore both the coincidence and the divergence of legal and moral rules. However, better candidates will provide discussion of a wide range of issues and will show understanding of the complex relationship between law and morality. It is important to consider the variety of ways in which the two can relate to each other. For example, the report on the January 2003 examination commented on the fact that not one candidate considered the possibility of legal rules influencing a change in moral rules.

Coincidence of legal and moral rules

Long-established legal rules influenced by moral rules

There are many long-established rules which have a moral connection. These include the laws of murder and theft, which can be traced back to the Ten Commandments.

Public morality may influence judicial change

Examples of this can be seen in criminal law, contract law and the law of tort.

Criminal law

- The decision in *R* v *R* (1991) was influenced by the moral rule that a husband should not be able to force his wife to have sexual intercourse. The law prior to this case had been representative of the attitude to marriage that prevailed until the latter part of the twentieth century.
- The decision in *R* v *Brown and others* (1993) was influenced by the moral rule that holds sado-masochistic activities as being unacceptable, even if consented to.

Contract law

In *Central London Property* v *High Trees House* (1965), Lord Denning created the equitable remedy of promissory estoppel. Prior to this, the common law had deemed that part payment would not settle a debt, even if the creditor promised it would. The remedy of promissory estoppel reflects the moral rule that people ought not to break their promises.

The law of tort

The decision in *Chadwick* v *British Railways* (1967) was influenced by the moral rule that people ought to help others who may be in trouble. A man who suffered nervous shock as a result of participation in a rescue operation was able to recover compensation and not required to satisfy the criteria that applied to other secondary victims.

Public morality may influence legislative reform

The major legislative reforms of the 1960s, particularly those concerning prostitution, abortion and homosexuality, could be said to reflect the 'permissive' moral ideals of that decade. Abortion was legalised by the **Abortion Act 1967** and the **Sexual Offences Act 1967** legalised homosexuality. As public morality has shifted towards a greater acceptance of homosexuality, the law has followed by reducing the age of consent. In 1994 the age of consent was reduced from 21 to 18, and in December 2000 it was reduced to 16.

Public morality may be influenced by law reform

It can be argued that some legislation is introduced partly with the aim of educating the public to consider certain matters unacceptable, i.e. morally wrong. An example of such legislation is that concerning discrimination, which aims to educate that to treat other people differently on the grounds of sex, race or disability is wrong.

Law reform may be the product of a campaign to change public morality

In 1949, the Howard League for Penal Reform persuaded the government to appoint a Royal Commission on Capital Punishment. The Howard League then persuaded most members of that Commission to be in favour of abolition of the death penalty. The government refused to implement the proposals because public opinion was such that it was considered to be morally correct to have the death penalty. Subsequently, a pressure group called the National Campaign for the Abolition of Capital Punishment was set up. During the years 1955–57, public opinion was changed by the campaign and the government introduced the necessary legislation to abolish the death penalty.

The pluralistic nature of society means coincidence is partial

In England, there is a large population of mixed cultures and races, of mixed political ideals and of differing religious followings. This leads to a significant divergence of views on a number of moral issues. For example, some people may argue that homosexuality between consenting males over the age of 16 is morally acceptable while others would disagree.

Similar arguments can be raised concerning the abortion issue. Some people will regard abortion as totally immoral. Others may feel that abortion is acceptable for medical reasons only. Even those who are not against abortion may disagree about the stage of pregnancy at which such a procedure is acceptable.

Indeed, it can be argued that there is no public moral consensus on any moral issue. Further examples to consider are:
- *Gillick* v *West Norfolk and Wisbech Area Health Authority* (1986). This concerned the prescription by doctors of contraceptives to girls under 16 without parental consent.

- *Re A (Children)* (2000). This arose out of a disagreement between doctors and the parents of Siamese twins on whether the doctors should operate to try and save the life of one of the twins. The case established the general defence of necessity, provided certain criteria applied:
  - the act was needed to avoid inevitable and irreparable evil
  - no more was done than was reasonably necessary for the purpose to be achieved
  - the evil inflicted was not disproportionate to the evil avoided

  The court decided that in the case of the twins the criteria were met and the defence could apply to what otherwise would be murder.
- The Dianne Pretty case (2001). This raised the issue of euthanasia and s.4 of the **Homicide Act 1957** regarding suicide pacts.

All these issues generated considerable debate, incorporating widely contrasting views. They illustrate the problem of trying to create legal rules in areas where there is no moral consensus.

Reasons for the overlap between legal and moral rules

There are several reasons for the broad overlap between legal and moral rules. Both aim to impose certain standards of conduct without which human society would break down. In many of these fundamental standards, law and morality reinforce and supplement each other as part of the fabric of social life.

It is therefore clear that legal rules do not exist in a vacuum, but, as Harris writes, 'are found side by side with moral codes of greater or less complexity. The relationship of law to moral rules and standards is therefore one of great and abiding importance in every human society, and certainly not least in our own'.

Moral codes, then, can be said to supplement and underpin the force of the legal rules which forbid immoral acts. The moral disapproval which such acts inspire is reinforced by the sanctions and remedies imposed by the law.

The close link between legal and moral rules is also demonstrated by the similarity of normative language that each employs. Both are concerned to lay down rules or 'norms' of conduct for human beings, and this is expressed in both moral and legal language in terms of obligations, duties, or of what is right or wrong.

Divergence of legal and moral rules

Some legal rules appear to have no moral connection

There appears to be little moral justification for the fact that tobacco and alcohol consumption are legal while smoking cannabis is illegal. Likewise, what is the moral justification for closing pubs at 11p.m.? And is it morally wrong to park on yellow lines or drive on a motorway at 72 miles per hour? There are some arguments, however, against the assertion that such laws have no connection with morals. It may be considered immoral, for example, to park in disabled parking spaces if you are not actually disabled or to partially block roads, making access difficult for emergency services vehicles.

Some moral rules have little or no legal backing

As considered on p.13, there is a moral duty to help those who may be in danger. The general position of the law, however, is that there is no liability for an omission to act. So, for example, the passer-by who fails to rescue someone who is drowning will not be held responsible. However, there are some exceptions in criminal law to this rule, such as where a person creates the danger, as in the case of *R v Miller* (1982), where there is an assumption of responsibility, where there is a special relationship and where there is a contractual duty to act.

The remedy of promissory estoppel (see p.14) is an exception to the general position of the law that there is no legal requirement to keep a promise. There is, however, a moral duty to do so.

Reasons for the divergence between legal and moral rules

As can be seen from the above examples, the law often shrinks from pursuing what may be recognised as the path of morality. The reasons for this vary. It may be because the moral attitude may not be sufficiently widespread, and the law would not reflect popular morality. It may also be because there are fields of human activity where the law deliberately prefers to abstain from supporting the moral rule because it is felt that the machinery of enforcement is too cumbersome to deal with the moral wrong — more social harm may be created than prevented by legal intervention. This was the reason why the Wolfenden Committee recommended that private homosexual behaviour should be decriminalised.

Natural law theorists

Natural law theorists argue that, in order to be valid, the law must coincide with natural law. During the past 2,500 years there have been many different views expressed as to what natural law is.

In the fourth century BC, the Greek philosopher Aristotle based his theory of natural law on the law of nature. He believed that the principles which governed the universe, and which explained how it was structured and how it functioned, could be discovered through observation and the power of human reason.

By the Middle Ages, natural law theorists believed that the natural law was the divine law or the law of God. St Thomas Aquinas, writing in the thirteenth century, expressed the view that the universe was created by God, and that when God created man he enabled him to know the truth. According to Aquinas, man is able to discover the truth of divine law through revelation, for example in the Holy Scriptures, through reflection, and through practical reasoning. Aquinas believed that if human law was at variance with the divine law, it was not legal but rather a corruption of the law.

In more recent times, the influence of the church has arguably declined. Professor Lon Fuller, in his book, *Morality of Law*, published in 1963, refers to what he terms the 'inner morality of law'. For Fuller, a legal system is only valid if it conforms to eight procedural requirements, these being that the laws must be:

- in existence and not made ad hoc
- published
- prospective, not retrospective
- understandable
- consistent
- possible to comply with
- not changed so frequently that people are unable to regulate their conduct by them
- administered by society in accordance with how they are announced

While it can be seen that views expressed as to what natural law is have varied and continue to vary, there is nevertheless a common thread. As Lord Lloyd of Hampstead points out in *Introduction to Jurisprudence*: 'What has remained constant is an assertion that there are principles of natural law...the essence of natural law may be said to lie in the constant assertion that there are objective moral principles which depend upon the nature of the universe and which can be discovered by reason.'

Positivists

Jeremy Bentham

Jeremy Bentham (1748–1832) rejected natural law theories as being 'nonsense upon stilts'. His key criticisms were that natural law was based upon unprovable principles, and that natural law theorists confused legal issues with moral issues. For Bentham, the validity of a law did not depend on whether it was good or bad. What the law is and what the law ought to be should be treated as different issues. Bentham was primarily concerned with the promotion of the utility principle, i.e. the greatest happiness for the greatest number, by which he believed that a law could be considered good or bad. However, a law adjudged to be bad would not automatically be adjudged to be invalid.

John Austin

John Austin (1790–1859) is credited with formulating the first coherent theory of positivism. He rejected the principle of natural law, whereby validity of law is dependent upon it not being in conflict with a 'higher law', be it natural or divine. For

Austin, a law may be valid irrespective of its moral content. He defined law in terms of a command from a sovereign, whom the bulk of society is in the habit of obeying, enforced by a sanction. The origins of the command theory can be traced to Bentham and to Hobbes (1588–1679).

H. L. A. Hart

Professor Hart, in his book *The Concept of Law*, published in 1963, also subscribes to the positivist view. However, he is critical of Austin's command theory in three respects. First, he argues that not all laws resemble orders backed by threats. For example, while this definition is true of criminal law, it is not relevant in contract law or family law, which confer powers on people so that they may arrange their personal affairs. Second, the requirement of the habit of obedience is impossible to apply when a new sovereign succeeds the old one. Third, Hart argues that in most states there are limitations on the legal powers of the sovereign.

The Hart–Fuller debate

The Hart–Fuller debate took place during the years 1958–67. In essence, it was a response of both natural law theory and positivism to the views expressed by the German philosopher Gustav Radbruch, on the validity of laws passed under the Nazi regime. Radbruch had been a positivist prior to the Nazi era, but the atrocities perpetrated, apparently with legal approval, during that period led him to believe that no law could be valid if it contravened basic moral principles.

Following the Second World War, many informers were tried as war criminals. In their defence they typically argued that what they were doing was legal, as the law at that time made it illegal to make statements which were detrimental to the government. The approach of the German courts was to declare these Nazi laws invalid as they were 'contrary to the sound conscience and sense of justice of all decent human beings'. This approach was clearly in agreement with the natural law theorists and Fuller supported it.

Hart disagreed with Fuller. According to Hart, the law was valid despite being so fundamentally contrary to moral principles. Hart did not disagree that the law was immoral, only that it was invalid.

The Hart–Devlin debate

The issue of how far law and morals should coincide was widely discussed in the late 1950s, when there was public concern about an apparent decline in sexual morality. This became known as the Hart–Devlin debate, not to be confused with the Hart–Fuller debate, which was concerned with the validity of legal rules that conflict with moral rules. The Hart–Devlin debate was concerned with the extent to which the law should enforce moral rules.

Statements reflecting the pluralistic nature of society can be found in the debates surrounding the legal reforms of the 1960s. The **Sexual Offences Act 1967**, which legalised homosexuality, was introduced following recommendations made by the Wolfenden Committee in its 1957 report. Two years after the publication of the Wolfenden Report, Lord Devlin, in his book, *The Enforcement of Morals*, set out his criticisms of the Wolfenden recommendations. In 1962, Professor Hart set out his arguments against Devlin's views in his book, *Law, Liberty and Morality*.

Professor Hart drew on the work of John Stuart Mill who, in his essay 'On liberty' (1859), stated: 'The only part of the conduct of anyone, for which he is amenable to society, is that which concerns others. In the part which merely concerns himself, his independence, is of right, absolute. Over himself, over his own body and mind, the individual is sovereign.' John Stuart Mill and Professor Hart put forward the view that the minority should not be made to conform to the will of the majority when in private, as this would amount to tyranny and be immoral. They thus recognised the pluralistic nature of society.

Professor Hart argued that using law to enforce moral values was unnecessary, undesirable and morally unacceptable: unnecessary because society was capable of containing many moral standpoints without disintegrating; undesirable because it would freeze morality at a particular point; and morally unacceptable because it infringes the freedom of the individual. He also pointed out that objections to unusual behaviour are often prompted by ignorance, prejudice and misunderstanding.

Sir James Stephen, a leading criminal judge in the late nineteenth century, disagreed with Mill. In his work *Liberty, Equality, Fraternity* (1874) he stated: 'I think that the attempt to distinguish between self-regarding acts and acts which regard others is like an attempt to distinguish between acts which happen in time and acts which happen in space. Every act happens at some time and in some space, and, in like manner, every act that we do either does or may affect both ourselves and others. I therefore think that the distinction is altogether fallacious and unfounded.' He went on to say: 'There are acts of wickedness so gross and outrageous that they must be punished at any cost to the offender.' Stephen's view was that the prevention of immoral behaviour was an end in itself.

Lord Devlin's views are more in line with those of Sir James Stephen. While Devlin believed that individual privacy should be respected, he stated: 'History shows that the loosening of moral bonds is often the first stage of disintegration...suppression of vice is as much the law's business as the suppression of subversive activities.' He believed that society shared a common morality and that the law should intervene to punish acts which offend that shared morality, whether done in public or private. Failure to intervene would result in the disintegration of society. He argued that individual liberty could only flourish in a stable society; disintegration of society through lack of a shared morality would, therefore, threaten individual freedom.

> **Tip**
>
> This debate must be discussed in relation to the coincidence of legal and moral rules. Better candidates will demonstrate detailed knowledge of the views of both Professor Hart and Lord Devlin, and will be able to explain how the debate has influenced the law in more recent years.

The influence of Mill–Hart

Sir John Wolfenden followed the views of Mill and Hart, recognising the pluralistic nature of society and the importance of individual liberty. The resulting legislation, the **Sexual Offences Act 1967**, legalising homosexuality, was thus influenced by the views of Mill and Hart. Their views were also reflected in other reforming legislation of that period such as the **Obscene Publications Act 1968** and the **Divorce Law Reform Act 1969**.

The majority of the House of Lords in *Gillick* v *Norfolk and Wisbech Area Health Authority* (1986) also adopted the Mill–Hart approach. They held that it was legal for doctors to offer contraceptive advice and treatment to girls under the age of 16, provided they were satisfied that the girls had sufficient understanding of the issues involved. The decision created what has become known as the 'Gillick competent child'. In Lord Scarman's words, the principle is that 'parental rights are derived from parental duty' and that the 'dwindling right' of a parent as the child grows older 'yields to the child's right to make his own decision when he reaches a sufficient understanding and intelligence to be capable of making up his own mind on the matter requiring decision'.

The influence of Stephen–Devlin

The dissenting judgements of Lords Brandon and Templeman in *Gillick* v *Norfolk and Wisbech Area Health Authority* (1986) reflected concerns over the wider social implications. Lord Brandon's dissent was based largely on the question of public policy and his concern for the criminal aspect in terms of under-age sex. Lord Templeman ignored case law and produced an opinion which read like a speech by Mrs. Gillick, the most memorable line of which is: 'There are many things which a girl under 16 needs to practise but sex is not one of them.' These views were an echo of Lord Devlin's concern about social disintegration.

The influence of Stephen and Devlin can be seen in a number of other judicial decisions. In *Shaw* v *DPP* (1962), the Ladies' Directory case, the House of Lords ruled that a publication advertising the services of prostitutes was a conspiracy to corrupt public morals. Viscount Simmonds argued: 'In the sphere of criminal law I entertain no doubt that there remains in the courts a residual power to enforce the supreme and fundamental purpose of the law, to conserve not only the safety and order, but also the moral welfare of the state.'

More recent decisions show that there is still judicial support for the Devlin viewpoint that some acts are intrinsically immoral, regardless of whether they harm others. In *Knuller* v *DPP* (1973), a case involving advertisements in a magazine placed by readers, inviting others to contact them for homosexual purposes, the decision in *Shaw* was followed. In *R* v *Gibson* (1990) an artist exhibited earrings made from freeze-dried fetuses of 3–4 months gestation. A conviction for the common law offence of outraging public decency was upheld.

Perhaps the most significant recent decisions are those of the House of Lords in *R* v *Brown and others* (1993) and the European Court of Human Rights in *Laskey, Brown and Jaggard* v *United Kingdom* (1997). In the House of Lords case, the question was whether the defence of consent could be used in respect of sadomasochistic acts. The people involved were consenting adults and none of the activities were conducted in public or had resulted in the need for medical treatment. The activities concerned included whipping, caning, branding and nailing their genitals to pieces of wood. The House of Lords held that the defence of consent could not be applied to such practices and that such behaviour was not to be encouraged by relaxation of the law. When the defendants took their case to the European Court of Human Rights they lost on the basis that there was no breach of Article 8, as infringement of the right to respect for private life was justified by the need to protect health or morals.

Conclusion

One of the difficulties for the law is that not only is society pluralistic, with a wide range of views on all moral issues, but also that these views are sometimes passionately held, allowing little scope for compromise. In general terms, it could be argued that a large section of society has come to adopt the view taken by Professor Hart, and inevitably this has been reflected in both legislative changes and in judicial decisions such as *Gillick*. On the other hand, significant groups remain opposed to what they perceive as a dangerous weakening of the moral basis of law.

Moral issues are always liable to figure prominently in the media and you are encouraged to use whatever examples are currently in the news. For example, in March 2005 the issue of abortion once again became prominent when Michael Howard, the leader of the Conservative Party, called for a lowering of the time limit for abortions from 24 weeks gestation to 20 weeks.

Besides abortion, other issues concerning the sanctity of life such as euthanasia, stem cell research and interventions in the field of human fertilisation remain contentious.

Another issue giving rise to strongly held views is that of fox hunting. In February 2005, the **Hunting Act 2004** became law, making hunting with dogs illegal. However, the issue looks likely to remain on the political agenda, with supporters of hunting seemingly determined to make the Act unworkable.

> **Tip**
>
> Better candidates will be able to discuss some of these issues in the context of the Hart–Devlin debate and will be able to make judgements about how far in practice law and morality are linked, and whether it is appropriate for the law to be used to resolve moral issues.

Law and justice

The meaning of 'justice'

'Justice' has many meanings. The definition given in the *Oxford English Dictionary* is 'just conduct; fairness', and this is the common understanding of the word. The definition of 'just' is 'acting or done in accordance with what is morally right or proper'. The definition of 'fair' is 'free from discrimination, dishonesty…in conformity with rules or standards'. Lord Lloyd emphasises the difficulty in defining justice precisely: 'Justice, whatever its precise meaning may be, is itself a moral value, that is one of the aims or purposes which man sets himself in order to attain the good life.' It would appear that conceptions of justice vary from age to age, person to person and according to existing economic relations.

While justice is simplified in the dictionary by the idea of 'fairness', C. H. Perelman recognised that justice has several meanings. In his book, *De La Justice* (1945), he set out six possible meanings of justice:

(1) 'To each according to his works' (rewards are based on contribution)
(2) 'To each according to his needs' (people receive what they need)
(3) 'To each according to his merits' (people get what they deserve)
(4) 'To each according to his rank' (people may enjoy privileges according to status)
(5) 'To each according to his legal entitlement' (people receive what the law says they should)
(6) 'To each equally' (all people receive the same)

While recognising that justice may have several meanings, Perelman believed that once the type of justice subscribed to by a society was identified, then all individuals had to be treated the same. He subscribed to the theory of formal justice.

Justice, according to the law, can be formal and/or substantive. Formal justice, often referred to as procedural justice, requires equality of treatment in accordance with the classification laid down by rules. Substantive justice is concerned with whether or not the actual rules are just.

> **Tip**
>
> Most exam questions will require you to explain in theory what justice is, and then to explain to what extent justice is achieved in practice. However, a common fault is to define justice well and to give examples of justice in operation, but not to link these two parts.

Theories of justice

There are numerous theories of justice. It is important to be able to explain and evaluate these theories and their relationships with each other, and to understand their application to modern society.

Aristotle

The Greek philosopher Aristotle introduced the principles of distributive justice and corrective justice:

- The principle of distributive justice requires that the allocation of assets in society should be proportional to a person's claim on them. He argued that this did not necessarily mean equal shares.
- The principle of corrective justice requires that where distributive justice is disturbed by wrongdoing, there should be a means of restoring the original position. This might be done by imposing penalties or awarding compensation.

St Thomas Aquinas

Aquinas's **natural law theory** makes the assumption that if higher law is followed, the result will be justice. An unjust law might be contrary to human good or against the higher law derived from God. A law which goes against this God-derived law will always be 'unjust' and should not be obeyed. Some Roman Catholics today would argue that this applies to laws legalising abortion. Members of many faith groups would find it difficult to obey laws that compelled them to break what they regard as fundamental principles. Interesting examples are the law in France forbidding the wearing of religious symbols in state institutions such as schools, and the exemption given to Sikhs in the UK from the requirement to wear a crash helmet when riding a motorcycle.

Jeremy Bentham

The **theory of utilitarianism** was developed by Jeremy Bentham. The aim of utilitarianism is to maximise human happiness by increasing pleasure and diminishing pain. For the utilitarian, justice is concerned with promoting 'the greatest happiness of the greatest number'. The sum of human happiness is assessed by numerical means and each person's happiness is equal in value.

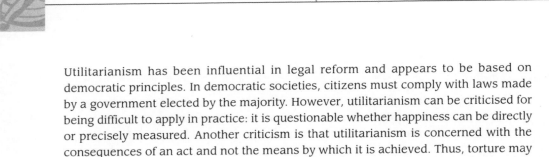

Utilitarianism has been influential in legal reform and appears to be based on democratic principles. In democratic societies, citizens must comply with laws made by a government elected by the majority. However, utilitarianism can be criticised for being difficult to apply in practice: it is questionable whether happiness can be directly or precisely measured. Another criticism is that utilitarianism is concerned with the consequences of an act and not the means by which it is achieved. Thus, torture may justify the end result of obtaining information. Individuals are not regarded as important and the complete misery of a few is justified if it increases the happiness of the many.

John Rawls

John Rawls in *A Theory of Justice* (1971) sets out justice as fairness:

> The 'main task clearly is to determine which principles of justice would be chosen in the original position...The idea of the original position is to set up a fair procedure so that any principles agreed to will be just...It seems reasonable to suppose that the parties in the original position are equal, that is, all have the same rights in the procedure for choosing principles; each can make proposals, submit reasons for their acceptance and so on....

In order to avoid the situation whereby people exploit social and natural circumstances to their own advantage, Rawls places these people in the original position behind a 'veil of ignorance', whereby 'the parties do not know certain kinds of particular facts. First of all, no one knows his place in society, his class position or social status; nor does he know his fortune in the distribution of natural assets and abilities, his intelligence and strength and the like'. Furthermore, people behind the veil of ignorance do not know what they will value as good or bad, or what economic or political situation, level of civilisation and culture are prevalent in their society. According to Rawls, two principles would be chosen from these circumstances: 'First: each person is to have an equal right to the most extensive basic liberty compatible with a similar liberty for others. Second: social and economic inequalities are to be arranged so that they are both (a) reasonably expected to be to everyone's advantage, and (b) attached to positions and offices open to all.'

Rawls rejects the notion of utility. He believes that justice is achieved through rules which create inequality only if that inequality is of benefit to all, not merely to the greatest number. Furthermore, the equal right to liberty cannot be denied in favour of greater social or economic advantages.

Rawls's theory of justice is reflected in both English law and in the European Convention on Human Rights. Rawls subscribes to liberalism, which is primarily concerned with freedom and the autonomy of individuals. The European Convention on Human Rights reflects this in that it ensures individuals are given the positive rights Rawls regards as important, including freedom of speech and assembly and freedom from arbitrary arrest and seizure. However, the derogation clauses depart from Rawls's theory, allowing for a denial of rights, for example 'in the interests of national security, public safety or the economic well-being of the country, for the prevention of disorder or crime, for the protection of health or morals, or for the protection of the rights and freedoms of others' (Article 8). Only the last point arguably reflects Rawls's theory, in that individual liberty can be limited if it will result in greater liberty overall.

Marxism

Karl Marx, like Rawls, subscribed to an ideal of justice rather than to an actual existing system. For Marx, the ideal society meant, 'From each according to his ability, to each according to his needs'. He argued that justice cannot be achieved until the ideal society is in place, for any other society is defective and justice therein impossible. However, Marx also propounded the view that: 'Once the new productive arrangements appear, there will be no need for principles of justice for production or distribution.' This implies that no one would find it necessary to rely upon institutional apparatus to recognise his or her rights. Justice for Marx would be the existence of his ideal society and there would apparently be no need for a law to conform to. Such sentiments were also expressed by eighteenth-century theorist **David Hume**: 'If every man had a tender regard for another, or if nature supplied abundantly all our wants and desires...the jealousy of interest, which justice supposes, could no longer have place. Increase to a sufficient degree the benevolence of men, or the bounty of nature, and you render justice useless.' It is clear that Britain does not correspond to the ideal society as envisaged by either Hume or Marx.

Robert Nozick and the minimal state

Nozick rejected the distributive theories of justice of Rawls and Marx and instead developed the **entitlement theory** of justice, according to which goods arise already encumbered with ownership. He maintained that individuals have natural rights to the enjoyment of life, health, liberty and possessions, free from interference by others. Rather than being concerned with equality, the entitlement theory stipulates that the state should only intervene to protect natural rights: inequalities are a fact of life. It holds that the state should play a minimum role and is not justified in diminishing or increasing the natural rights which an individual possesses. Redistribution of individuals' rights is not justified for any social purpose. Legal systems such as that operating in the UK, which go further than merely enforcing natural rights, do not comply with Nozick's theory of justice.

The extent to which substantive legal rules, legal institutions and processes achieve justice

> **Tip**
>
> In questioning whether the English law complies with the requirements of formal and substantive justice, examples of rules, institutions and processes from many parts of the specification can be used. These examples can then be related to the meanings and theories of justice and examined in order to assess how successful they are in achieving justice.

Natural justice and the rule of law

It would be reasonable to claim that if a legal system is to be based on justice, it must incorporate the principles of natural justice and the rule of law.

Phil Harris, in *An Introduction to Law*, argues that the idea of natural justice 'has no mysterious or magical meaning: it simply refers to a duty to act fairly'. This is based on two requirements: that each party should have the opportunity to be heard and that no one should be judge in his own cause. This principle can be seen operating in *R v Bow Street Metropolitan Stipendiary Magistrate, ex parte Pinochet* (1999), in which the House of Lords decided that General Pinochet, the former dictator of Chile, should be extradited to Spain to face serious charges of human rights abuse. When it was revealed that Lord Hoffman, one of the Law Lords who heard the case, had links with Amnesty International, a human rights organisation involved in the proceedings, the House of Lords annulled the decision and reheard the case without Lord Hoffman.

The theory of the rule of law as outlined by Dicey in the nineteenth century is that 'no person is punishable except for a distinct breach of the law established in the courts' and also that no man is 'above the law, but that every man, whatever his rank, is subject to the ordinary law of the realm'.

Judicial review

One of the ways in which the rule of law is guaranteed is by having an independent judiciary able to review the decisions of politicians and public officials.

The system of judicial review does not examine the merits of a decision, but simply whether the body or individual in question was within their rights in making the decision. If a decision is *ultra vires* (goes beyond their powers), it can be quashed. Procedural *ultra vires* arises where proper procedures have not been followed, e.g. there has been a breach of natural justice, as in the Pinochet case. Substantive *ultra vires* arises where the content of the decision was outside the power of the body that made it. One of the problems with substantive *ultra vires* is that it is difficult for judges to control the actions of public bodies if the discretionary powers granted to such bodies are very wide. For example, in *R v Secretary of State for the Environment ex parte Norwich City Council* (1982), the wording of the **Housing Act 1980** allowed the Secretary of State to 'do all such things as appear to him necessary or expedient' to enable council house tenants to buy their council houses. The courts accepted that, in cases where sales were proceeding slowly, this gave him the right to remove the power from the local authority and exercise it himself.

It could be argued that the real test of whether a system is based on the principles of justice is how it copes with direct or perceived threats to the security of the state. It has been suggested that the reliance by governments on the requirements of national security has inhibited judicial review of their decisions. In *R v Secretary of State for Home Affairs ex parte Hosenball* (1977), the Court of Appeal held that an American journalist could be deported, even though the rules of natural justice had not been followed, because the decision was made on the grounds of national security. Similarly, in *Council of Civil Service Unions v Minister for the Civil Service* (1984), the government decision to ban employees at the Government Communications Headquarters (GCHQ) from membership of trade unions was upheld on the basis that it claimed that it was necessary for reasons of national security.

However, the passing of the **Human Rights Act 1998** has enabled judges to review even primary legislation to determine whether it complies with the European Convention on Human Rights. In *A and others v Secretary of State for the Home Department* (2004), the House of Lords took the view that the detention of foreign nationals without trial under s.21 of the **Anti-terrorism, Crime and Security Act 2001** was not justified, even though the government argued that they were a threat to national security.

The government has responded to this judicial decision by releasing the detainees, but under control orders greatly restricting their freedom. It has also secured new legislation (**Prevention of Terrorism Act 2005**) allowing for the use of such control orders in the future for both British and foreign terror suspects. It remains to be seen whether this legislation will be challenged under the **Human Rights Act**. It would appear that judges are now more ready to uphold the rights of unpopular individuals and require that the rules of natural justice be followed despite the national security argument.

Access to justice

The rules relating to equal access to justice in England seem to have become more substantially unjust in recent years. Government funding for legal cases was introduced by the **Legal Aid Act 1949**, with the aim of providing the means for everyone to have access to justice, rather than only those who could afford it. The system was means-tested and demand-led so that all those who applied would receive funding, provided they fell within the eligibility criteria. When the system was first introduced, approximately 80% of the population were eligible for some government funding; however, the expense to the taxpayer of this system persuaded successive governments to alter the means test so that fewer people qualified, and by the early 1990s only 40% of the population were eligible for legal aid. The majority of the population fell into what was referred to as the 'middle income trap': too rich to qualify for legal aid yet too poor to fund legal action themselves.

The position has been improved to some extent by the **Access to Justice Act 1999**, but problems remain. The Act introduced a limit on the amount of funding available, so that when the money runs out, no funding is available. The limits for eligibility remain low. There are also certain types of action excluded from the system, such as personal injury cases, although these can be pursued through conditional fee arrangements. However, not all of those who may have qualified for legal aid under the old system can find a lawyer willing to accept their case on a conditional fee. Lawyers are only willing to accept those cases they feel sure of winning. All of these issues mean that some people have access to the legal system, while others do not.

The rules regarding government funding suggest that formal justice is denied. The law in general cannot be applied impartially if certain sections of society are denied access to it. It can also be argued that such rules are substantially unjust because they have the effect of denying equal access.

The civil justice system

The civil justice system as it operated before 1999 was widely criticised as being unfair. Elliott and Quinn, in *The English Legal System*, comment that: 'While conflicting interests may mean it is impossible to achieve a civil justice system that satisfies everyone, there were serious concerns that the civil justice system before April 1999 was giving satisfaction to only a small minority of users.'

Lord Woolf, in his final report published in 1996, identified a number of goals which a civil justice system should have. The first two of these were that it should be just in the results it delivers and fair in the way it treats litigants. The changes proposed by Woolf were implemented in the **Civil Procedure Rules 1999**. He described these as 'a new landscape for civil justice for the twenty-first century' and they certainly represent a significant reform. The overriding objective in the rules, with their emphasis on pre-action protocols and pro-active case management by judges, is that the courts should deal with cases justly and that this objective is to prevail over all others.

The new system has generally been welcomed as an improvement, although the reforms were described by Michael Zander, a leading academic, as being 'fundamentally flawed'. For example, he points out that procedural timetables for the fast track may not work fairly because lawyers, for a variety of reasons, may not be able to keep to the prescribed timetables. This could result in sanctions being imposed on parties deemed to have caused the delays, thus punishing them for what in effect are the failings of their lawyers.

The criminal justice system

The miscarriage of justice cases in the 1980s and 1990s, such as the Guildford Four, the Maguires and the Birmingham Six, raised questions about the way the criminal justice system was operating and suggested that in their eagerness to get convictions in what were dreadful murders, the police had been prepared to compromise some of the principles of formal justice. In particular, there were concerns about confessions and the treatment of the defendants while they were in custody and also about the reliability of forensic evidence.

When Judith Ward was cleared in 1992 after serving 18 years for the bombing of a coach on the M62 motorway, which killed 12 people, the Court of Appeal said that a grave miscarriage of justice had occurred:

> In failing to disclose evidence ...the West Yorkshire police, the scientists who gave evidence at the trial, and some of those members of the staff of the DPP and counsel who advised them ... failed to carry out their basic duty to seek to ensure a trial which is fair to both the prosecution ...and the accused.

Arguably, however, the system did eventually deliver justice, because the appeal system led to the convictions in all these IRA cases, and in others, such as the Tottenham Three and the Bridgewater Four, being quashed and compensation being paid.

Justice for victims?

The Stephen Lawrence case demonstrates that there can also be concerns about whether the institutions of the state operate fairly in the interests of all those affected by crime. Stephen Lawrence was murdered in an apparently racially motivated attack in 1993. The Macpherson Inquiry was set up by the government, as a result of concerns expressed about the way the police handled the case, and it concluded that the investigation was 'marred by a combination of professional incompetence, institutional racism and a failure of leadership by senior officers'. In this case, it is clear that Stephen's family feels an enormous sense of injustice, compounded by the fact that a private prosecution brought against the three men suspected of killing Stephen failed. Victims, unlike defendants, do not get a second chance and the recognition that those acquitted of Stephen's murder could not be tried again, regardless of any new evidence that might emerge, led to calls for the 'double jeopardy' rule to be relaxed. As a result, the **Criminal Justice Act 2003** allows for people acquitted of certain serious offences, including murder, to be retried, providing both the DPP and the Court of Appeal are satisfied that there is 'new and compelling evidence' and that it is in the interests of justice to have a retrial. The relevant clauses became law in April 2005.

The more recent case of Damilola Taylor also focuses on the sense of frustration felt by the families of victims when there are unsuccessful prosecutions. The response of some of the press to the acquittal of the defendants in that case suggested in the words of the _Daily Mirror_ was that this was 'another murdered black boy betrayed by

British justice'. But David Pannick in an article in *The Times* (7 May, 2002) argued that although 'justice was battered and bruised by the Taylor case', it survived the ordeal. He pointed out that 'show trials' do not take place in Britain and that justice can be served when defendants are acquitted because the jury is not satisfied of guilt beyond reasonable doubt. He also claimed that although mistakes were made, 'none of the errors of which the police have been accused in the Taylor case could, if avoided, have resulted in a conviction'.

Substantive criminal law: the defence of provocation

Provocation is a special defence to murder. If pleaded successfully, it will result in a conviction for voluntary manslaughter. The aim of the partial defences of provocation and diminished responsibility is to provide substantive justice, whereby those who kill but are not fully responsible for their actions are not found guilty of murder. The provocation defence has been topical in recent years due to the perceived unfairness it affords to women. The problem is the requirement set out in *R v Duffy* (1949) for a 'sudden and temporary loss of self control'. It has become apparent that the general impartial application of this defence results in injustice to women who, by virtue of their comparative strength with their husbands, are less likely to act spontaneously and be able to rely on the strict interpretation of the defence. This has been mitigated to a certain extent by *R v Ahluwalia* (1993), in which battered woman syndrome was regarded as evidence of the 'abnormality of mind' required under the defence of diminished responsibility. Clearly, there is still a need for some reform of this defence before it can be regarded as substantially just. The Ahluwalia decision in effect typecasts battered women as mentally impaired, having to rely on the defence of diminished responsibility, unlike apparently legally sane males who may rely on the provocation defence.

One proposal which has been put forward by the Labour peer Lord Ashley is to abolish the need for sudden loss of control. Another is to create a new defence of self preservation, which would apply to both men and women, but which would take into account the way in which women react, and allow a defence to women like Ahluwalia, who kill out of fear but not in the heat of the moment. Critics of this proposal argue that it would create a licence to kill. It is questionable whether the proposed defence would result in more justice or would simply change the balance of injustice.

Substantive criminal law: the defence of intoxication

This defence is useful in the context of justice because it illustrates the difficulty the law has in striking a balance which is fair to both victim and defendant. Currently, involuntary intoxication is a defence to specific but not basic intent crimes. It is clear that there is a problem here with applying the principles of justice. Formal justice requires consistency in the way rules operate and yet we treat basic and specific intent in different ways. The illogical nature of this approach is apparent. If intoxication can prevent a person forming a specific intent, it can surely also prevent someone recognising a risk and therefore being reckless. There is thus the potential injustice that someone can be found guilty even though they are clearly unable to form the *mens rea* for even a basic intent crime.

This problem was recognised by the House of Lords in *DPP* v *Majewski* (1977), but it firmly resisted the idea that intoxication should become a general defence, because this would be socially undesirable. Lord Salmon argued that while he accepted that there was 'a degree of illogicality in the rule that intoxication may excuse...one type of intention and not another...absolute logic in human affairs is an uncertain guide and a very dangerous master'. One important aspect of individual liberty, he argued, was protection against physical violence, and because the intoxication rule helped to achieve this 'the rule works without imperilling justice'.

Conclusion

It is clear that there are aspects of English law where the requirement for formal justice has not been met. This is also true of substantive justice, although arguably less so. However, a balanced view would point out that legislative reform such as the **Human Rights Act 1998** and the **Access to Justice Act 1999** have helped to ensure that procedures are more fair and individuals more likely to experience justice. Arguably, substantive justice does underpin the English legal system, and in the miscarriage of justice cases, for example, it was not the substantive law that was in question but the manner in which it was being administered.

It remains true, of course, that substantive law can be changed through enactment, so that laws regarded as unjust can be repealed. It is not so simple, however, to alter the behaviour of those administering the legal system.

Balancing conflicting interests

Theorists

There are several important theorists who ought to be considered in the issue of balancing conflicting interests and whether the law is effective in achieving this.

Karl Marx

Karl Marx (1818–83) believed that law was part of the 'repressive state apparatus' used to ensure the continuing exploitation of the working class (proletariat) by the capitalists (bourgeoisie), i.e. those who own the capital and means of production. For Marx, the law subordinated the interests of the proletariat to those of the bourgeoisie and so did not truly balance conflicting interests. Marx adhered to the conflict model of society and thus was of the view that law did not reconcile conflicting interests in a compromise but rather imposed the interest of one at the expense of another.

Rudolf von Jhering

Rudolf von Jhering (1818–92) believed that the law was a prime method of ordering society. Von Jhering was a utilitarian and more concerned with social than individual aims. His thinking followed that of Jeremy Bentham, whose principle of utility was aimed at maximising human happiness by increasing pleasure and diminishing pain according to the principle of 'the greatest happiness of the greatest number'. He saw society as made up of several competing interests, not all of which could be satisfied. He believed that the interests of the individual would conflict with the interests of society as a whole. The role of the law was to balance interests by reconciling the interests of the individual to society so that they conformed. This was achieved through state-organised coercion, i.e. the law, rewards, duty and love.

Roscoe Pound

Roscoe Pound (1870–1964) divided interests into two main categories: individual interests and social interests. He argued that interests could only be properly balanced if placed on the same plane or level. Thus social interests can be weighed against social interests and individual interests against individual interests. Failure to do this results in a built-in bias in favour of the social interest. Pound thus developed the ideas of von Jhering. He saw law as being developed according to social needs and only serving those interests that lead to the good of society. He subscribed to the consensus model of society, believing that interests should be balanced in accordance with society's values or 'jural postulates'.

In practice, this view does not seem to have been followed. For example, in the classic case of *Miller* v *Jackson* (1977), involving an application for an injunction against a cricket club by residents whose properties adjoined the cricket ground, Lord Denning approached the problem in terms of 'a conflict between the interest of the public at large and the interests of a private individual'. Denning concluded that the public interest outweighed the individual one and refused to grant the injunction, although he did attempt to balance this by awarding damages to compensate for the inconvenience of having cricket balls regularly hit into your garden.

To have followed Pound would have necessitated seeing both interests in the same terms, either as individual interests (one person's desire to play cricket against another person's desire to sit in his/her garden) or as social interests (the value to society of protecting domestic privacy against the value of encouraging recreational activities).

The courts have not generally adopted Pound's approach and many of the examples in this guide show the law attempting to balance what are perceived as valuable social interests against the rights of individuals.

Balancing of conflicting interests by Parliament

Legislative process

The balancing of competing interests is to some extent achieved by the process of making an Act of Parliament. The Green Paper invites consultation from various interested parties who may be affected by the proposed legislation. The bill stage of making the legislation requires many debates and votes. There are several political parties reflecting a wide range of views. Before the bill becomes an Act, many compromises and amendments will be made, which take into account the different views of those who are both interested and involved in the legislative process.

It is, however, questionable as to whether or not a true balance of conflicting interests is actually achieved by the legislative process. There are many powerful interest groups and classes within society. These groups influence the view of ministers, members of Parliament and civil servants. Many politicians are wealthy and influential. They may possess large shareholdings in companies and have directorships or other connections. They may be persuaded more often than they should by groups who are in favour of protecting such interests, despite requirements that these interests should be revealed.

Protective legislation

Parliament sometimes seeks to balance competing interests by passing laws which are advantageous to the weaker interest groups and disadvantageous to the powerful groups. Examples of such protective legislation can be seen in consumer law. The **Consumer Protection Act 1987** imposes strict liability on producers in respect of damage caused by dangerous products. The **Sale and Supply of Goods Act 1994** applies conditions to consumer contracts in respect of title, description, quality and sale by sample. By virtue of the **Unfair Contract Terms Act 1977**, the use of exclusion and limitation clauses by businesses in consumer contracts is significantly reduced.

However, while the provisions contained in protective legislation clearly aim to strengthen the weaker interest groups, it is questionable how successful such legislation is. Phil Harris, in *An Introduction to Law*, points out that such legislation is not rigorously enforced by the state. This, he argues, results in the protective legislation aiding the stronger group while appearing to aid the weaker one. The perceived protection offered to consumers enables businesses to enjoy a better public image and so further their own interests.

A further problem with consumer legislation is that it depends on enforcement by the consumer. Harris believes that most consumers are ignorant of the rights given to them by such legislation. For example, a shop may tell a customer who has purchased a faulty product that his or her only hope is to deal with the manufacturer direct, or that he or she is only entitled to a credit note, when this is not the case. He also questions whether the average customer would know that a clause in an agreement excluding liability for implied terms is invalid under the **Unfair Contract Terms Act 1977** (UCTA). Consumers who are aware of their rights may bring an action for breach of contract. Most such actions will usually need to be brought in the small claims court, for which there is no state assisted funding for legal representation. The result will often be that the protective legislation is not enforced, because even those consumers who are aware of their rights will consider legal action to be more trouble and expense than it is worth.

Balancing of conflicting interests by the courts

Judges are more obviously faced with balancing competing interests in the courts. Examples of law which may be referred to here include nuisance, occupiers' liability, crime and consumer law. In the law of nuisance, the claimant's interest in being able to enjoy his or her property must be balanced against the interest of his or her neighbours to do what they like with theirs. In occupiers' liability, the interests of the occupier of land have to be balanced against those who come onto their land. In crime, the interests of the offender have to be balanced against those of society, and in consumer law, the interests of the consumer have to be balanced against the interests of the business.

Public interests usually outweigh private interests

Pound's theory was that genuine balancing of conflicting interests could only be achieved when the interests were placed in the same category. It is apparent that if the interests in *Miller* v *Jackson* (1977) had been placed in the same category, the outcome may have been different. The interests could have both been placed in the individual category, i.e. Mr Miller's interests in privacy against Mr Jackson's personal interest in playing cricket, or they could have both been placed in the social category, i.e. the public interest in domestic privacy against the public interest in playing cricket.

Protection of national security is another social interest which nearly always prevails if balanced against an individual interest. Judges regard protection of national security as paramount. In *Council of Civil Service Unions* v *Ministry for the Civil Service* (1984), the GCHQ case, the prime minister issued an order under which workers at the intelligence-gathering centre were no longer permitted to belong to a trade union. The House of Lords backed the prime minister's order as it was made in the interest of national security, despite the valid argument of the unions that they had not been consulted. When Tony Blair became prime minister, he restored the right of workers to belong to a trade union, so the original threat to national security posed by such membership appears doubtful.

Public interest also outweighs private interest when the courts are required to balance one individual's right to respect for his private life, enshrined in Article 8 of the European Convention on Human Rights, and another's right to freedom of expression, enshrined in Article 10. Under the **Human Rights Act 1998** s.12(4), courts are now required to consider the extent to which it would be in the public interest to publish material which the claimant alleges would breach his or her right to respect for his or her private life.

Public interest further outweighs private interest in respect of most positive rights provided by the European Convention on Human Rights and the **Human Rights Act 1998**. Most of these rights are subject to derogation clauses, which are sometimes drafted in broad terms. Under Article 8, everyone has the right to respect for his private and family life, his home and his correspondence. However, Article 8 also expressly provides that this right can be overridden 'in the interests of national security, public safety or the economic well-being of the country, for the prevention of disorder or crime, for the protection of health or morals, or for the protection of the rights and freedoms of others'. Thus it seems that the rights of individuals will not prevail in the event of a conflict with the public interest.

However, while even the right to life is subject to qualification, some rights, including the right not to be subjected to torture or to inhuman or degrading treatment or punishment as provided by Article 3, are non-derogable.

A and others v Secretary of State for the Home Department (2004) provides a recent example of the courts deciding in favour of the private interest. The House of Lords decided that the use of s.21 of the **Anti-terrorism, Crime and Security Act 2001** to detain foreign nationals without charging them was unlawful and an infringement of their human rights. Despite the public interest arguments put forward by the Home Secretary, the Law Lords were willing recognise the importance of preserving private interests.

The willingness of juries to subordinate national security to other public interests

Jurors are not part of the permanent state machinery of enforcement. Perhaps, as a result, they are more willing than judges to question claims made by the executive or legislature of threats to national security. In *R v Ponting* (1984), a civil servant was charged under the **Official Secrets Act 1911** for leaking information about the sinking of the *Belgrano*, an Argentinian ship, during the Falklands War. Ponting argued that leaking the information was in the public interest because it showed that the British government had not been telling the truth. The judge said that Ponting's argument was no defence. The jury took a different view and acquitted him.

The civil courts and access to justice

Interests can only be balanced if there are institutions available to which aggrieved parties have access on an equal basis. The operation of the rule of law, state assisted funding of legal actions and the independence of the judiciary ensure that, in theory at least, the court and tribunal system is able to achieve balance.

However, the findings of the Woolf commission provide ample evidence that the civil courts often operate in ways which favour powerful organisations and disadvantage individual claimants. It could be argued that tribunals provide a fairer balance in that they have less formal procedures and encourage claimants to represent themselves. However, the ordinary claimant is likely to be facing an opponent who is represented, e.g. an employer or a government department, and this puts him or her at a significant disadvantage. Research by Genn and Genn in 1989 found that much of the law in tribunals was complex and technical. The small claims procedure is also designed to achieve greater balance between the parties and, as with the tribunal system, the emphasis is on informality. But again, there is evidence that the balance remains in favour of the parties who can afford to use lawyers. The majority of cases are brought by businesses trying to recover bad debts rather than by individual claimants.

Balancing conflicting interests in criminal law

Criminal law is concerned with balancing the interests of the offender with those of society. This can be evidenced both in criminal procedure and in the substantive criminal law.

Criminal procedure

The interest of society is the conviction of the guilty and the acquittal of the innocent. The interest of the defendant is to have an assumption of innocence, to be treated with dignity and to have a fair trial. There is also the interest of the victim to consider. The traditional balance of the law in favour of the defendant may leave victims feeling that their interests are not being effectively represented in the criminal process.

There are many aspects that could be considered here and much specific detail can be drawn from Unit 2. Of particular importance are the **Criminal Procedure and Investigation Act 1996**, which allows for the retrial of someone acquitted by a jury where there is evidence of intimidation of witnesses, and the **Criminal Justice Act 2003**, which gives the Court of Appeal the power to order a retrial where 'new and compelling evidence' comes to light after someone has been found not guilty.

In addition, there is the whole issue that surrounds the rights of defendants — burden of proof, rules on arrest, rules of evidence, right to silence, effect of not-guilty finding — and how these rules are designed to create balance between the prosecution and the defence. It is important to address the question of whether the balance has now swung too far in favour of the prosecution, and to look at the right to silence and the effect of s.34 of the **Criminal Justice and Public Order Act 1994,** which allow juries or magistrates to draw inferences from a defendant failing to mention, when under caution, facts later relied on in his defence. Also of relevance in this respect are sections 36 and 37, which deal with a defendant's failure, when being questioned, to account for objects in his possession, marks on his clothing or his presence at a particular place. Another example is the issue of whether an accused person should be entitled to bail. The **Bail Act 1976** created a presumption in favour of bail. The courts are obliged to grant bail unless one of the exceptions applies, i.e. unless there are substantial grounds for believing that the accused might commit another offence, interfere with witnesses, fail to fulfil the bail conditions or otherwise obstruct the cause of justice. This Act seeks to ensure the liberty of the accused until the trial. The court has to balance the interest of the public in being protected and the interest of the individual in being presumed innocent until proven guilty. There has been a shift towards the public interest in recent years, with legislation increasingly providing circumstances in which bail may or must be refused.

In each of these areas of criminal law, recent developments have therefore involved restricting the rights of defendants and placing greater emphasis on the interests of society and the victims of crime.

Substantive criminal law: the defence of intoxication

The public interest lies in being protected from those who cause harm when drunk. The individual interest lies in being held less responsible for actions carried out while intoxicated (and thus with limited *mens rea*) than for actions carried out with full awareness.

The availability of the defence of intoxication varies according to circumstances. Where the accused is involuntarily intoxicated, intoxication can be a defence to any crime, provided the accused lacks the necessary *mens rea*. It can be used as a defence to sections 20 and 47 of the **Offences Against the Person Act 1861**. Voluntary intoxication, however, can only be a defence to a crime of specific intent. The reasoning for this is that the courts regard voluntary intoxication as reckless in itself and recklessness is the level of *mens rea* required for crimes of basic intent. In *DPP* v *Majewski* (1977), the House of Lords refused to allow intoxication to be used as a defence to a basic intent offence. Lord Steyn said that one of the prime purposes of the criminal law is the protection from unprovoked violence of people who are pursuing their lawful lives; to allow intoxication as a defence would be to leave the citizen unprotected from such violence. The House of Lords firmly resisted the idea that intoxication should become a general defence, because this would be socially undesirable and would not provide a proper balance between the interests of the defendant and the interests of society as a whole.

Similarly in *R* v *O'Grady* (1987), the Court of Appeal said that the principle that a person should not be penalised for an honest mistake gave way to the consideration that society should be protected from those who do dangerous things as a result of intoxication.

The concept of strict liability

This is a departure from the general principle of English law that there should be no liability without fault. In the creation of strict liability crimes, the law may suppress the interests of the individual in the interest of public safety. The **Rivers (Prevention of Pollution) Act 1951** makes it a criminal offence to pollute rivers, without the need to prove such pollution is caused intentionally, recklessly or negligently. In *Alphacell* v *Woodward* (1972) the defendants were found guilty of polluting a river, despite the fact that they were not negligent and were unaware of the mechanical breakdown of their equipment, which usually prevented such pollution occurring. One justification for strict liability in situations like this is that it works to the disadvantage of the more powerful interest and thus helps to achieve balance.

Balancing conflicting interests in the law of tort

The law of tort is mainly concerned with balancing two individual interests. However, public interests sometimes arise, as seen earlier when considering *Miller* v *Jackson* (1977). In that case, the public interest was considered when determining whether to award an injunction.

Negligence

The interest of one individual in not being harmed through another's carelessness has to be balanced against the interest of the other individual in not being held liable for unforeseeable and remote consequences.

In the law on psychiatric injury, the law limits liability to secondary victims by applying stringent criteria not applied to primary victims. Primary victims, e.g. those directly involved in an accident, can clearly be foreseen as being likely to be affected by the defendant's actions. However, the courts apply restrictions on who can claim as a result of seeing or hearing something happen to someone else. To claim as a secondary victim, a person must prove five additional criteria:

(1) he or she is a person of ordinary phlegm
(2) he or she has close ties of love and affection with those in the accident
(3) he or she is close in time and space
(4) he or she perceived the accident with his or her own unaided senses
(5) it can be shown that psychiatric illness rather than just physical injury was foreseeable

These criteria were clarified in *Alcock* v *Chief Constable of South Yorkshire* (1991) and *Page* v *Smith* (1994). Victims who cannot satisfy all these criteria are not regarded by the law as having proximity of relationship with the defendant and are thus unforeseeable claimants.

These are difficult decisions to make and whether a true balancing of conflicting interests is achieved is questionable. The trauma of a person identifying a body in a mortuary or seeing an accident on television could be just as great as a qualifying claimant, but the court has to consider the interests of the defendant as well. It is arguably not fair to allow claims from people not directly involved in the accident, unless they are foreseeable claimants.

The rule on remoteness of damage as established in *The Wagon Mound* (1961) requires that the damage must be of a foreseeable type if the defendant is to be held liable for it. In this case, damage by fire was not a type of damage foreseeable as a result of oil being discharged into the sea. Had the damage been fouling by the oil, the claimant may have recovered compensation. Again, the courts struck a balance on the basis of foreseeability.

Nuisance

The law of private nuisance is clearly concerned with balancing the interests of one individual against another. It involves the competing interests of neighbours to enjoy their property. The law of nuisance allows for a certain amount of give and take, but maintains that unreasonable interference is unlawful. In deciding whether the level of interference is unreasonable, the courts take into account factors such as locality, sensitivity and malice. When considering the locality issue, the courts will decide whether a normally acceptable activity is merely being carried on in the wrong place. This was the situation in *Laws* v *Florinplace Ltd* (1981), when a shop in a residential area was converted into a sex shop and cinema club. The sensitivity issue arises when someone puts their land to unusual delicate use. He or she cannot then complain when it is affected by normal activities. However, if a sensitive claimant brings an action against a malicious defendant, as was the case in *Hollywood Silver Fox Farm* v *Emmett* (1936), the interests of the claimant prevail. The claimant bred mink. Mink eat their young when frightened. The defendant objected to the claimant's use of land and therefore fired shots near to the claimant's land. This would not usually constitute a nuisance but the defendant had deliberately set out to cause harm and so was held liable.

Tip

For the examination, candidates are expected to explore a variety of ways in which the law seeks to achieve a balancing of conflicting interests. Better candidates will consider both the law made by the legislature and the decisions made by the courts, and also the processes by which such laws are made. The interests which are being balanced should be clearly identified — a frequent omission of weaker candidates. Examples to illustrate the balancing of conflicting interests can be taken from virtually any part of the law specification.

Fault

The meaning of 'fault'

There are various definitions of 'fault'. The *Concise Oxford Dictionary* provides many definitions: 'defect, imperfection, blemish, of character...thing wrongly done...responsibility for something wrong...blame'. The *Collins Concise Dictionary* provides similar definitions: 'responsibility for a mistake or misdeed...guilty of error, culpable...blame'. Blameworthy is defined as 'deserving censure' (*COD*) or 'deserving blame' (*CCD*). Blame is defined in similar terms to fault with reference to responsibility, fault, culpability and responsibility.

While there are various definitions of fault, perhaps the core meaning is 'responsibility'. The definition, 'responsibility for something wrong', would appear to be the most useful for the purposes of discussing the role of fault in English law.

Fault in criminal law

Actus reus

To be found guilty of most criminal offences, an *actus reus* and *mens rea* must be present. The *actus reus*, meaning 'prohibited act', is made up of the acts, circumstances and consequences of a specific offence. It comprises the physical elements of the crime. In order to be found guilty of a criminal offence, the accused must commit the *actus reus* voluntarily. If the accused is not in control of his or her own actions for any reason, then he or she cannot be said to be acting voluntarily or at fault. There are criminal defences, including automatism and duress, which the accused may plead in such circumstances, proof of which will result in acquittal. The accused will thus not be held responsible for actions which are not the result of his or her rational will.

Automatism arises when someone suffers total loss of control due to external factors. In *R* v *Bailey* (1983) the accused, a diabetic, was charged under s.18 of the **Offences Against the Person Act 1861** after he hit his ex-girlfriend's new boyfriend on the head with an iron bar. He successfully claimed the defence of automatism. He had been in a hypoglycaemic state brought about by a failure to eat after drinking some sugar and water.

Mens rea

The *mens rea* is the mental element of the criminal offence and will usually be defined in terms of intention or recklessness. The state of mind required for a conviction will vary from one offence to another.

Intention can be either direct, where the purpose of the accused is to bring about the prohibited consequence, or oblique, where the accused recognises the result is a virtual certainty.

Recklessness can be defined as unjustified risk-taking and is now always considered as subjective following the important House of Lords judgement in *R* v *G* (2004), which abolished Caldwell recklessness, which had included some objective elements. Subjective recklessness requires the defendant knowingly to take a risk.

Murder and voluntary manslaughter

Murder is the most serious homicide offence and this fact is reflected in the mandatory sentence of life imprisonment issued for it. The accused must have had the intention to kill or to cause grievous bodily harm.

Partial defences to murder are contained in the **Homicide Act 1957** and, if proven, allow the court to find the accused guilty of the lesser crime of voluntary manslaughter. These partial defences, notably diminished responsibility and provocation, apply to situations where the accused is considered not to be totally in control of what he or she is doing. The defences thus recognise that such defendants are less at fault than murderers and so should be less liable for the consequences of their actions. The less serious nature of voluntary manslaughter is recognised through the life sentence being discretionary rather than mandatory.

Under s.3 of the **Homicide Act 1957**, the defence of provocation requires proof that provocative conduct caused the defendant to lose self-control, and that a reasonable person would have reacted in the same way. In *DPP* v *Camplin* (1978), the murder conviction was reduced to voluntary manslaughter on the basis of provocation. The accused was 15 years old. He killed his victim by hitting him over the head with a chapatti pan after the victim had homosexually assaulted him and then taunted him about it.

Involuntary manslaughter

Involuntary manslaughter is much more difficult to classify in terms of fault. Now that the definition of recklessness is clearly subjective, it is hard to see how the objective test in the definition of 'dangerous' in unlawful and dangerous act manslaughter can be justified. The definition of 'dangerous' is that given in *R* v *Church* (1966) as meaning 'in the sense that a sober and reasonable person would inevitably recognise that it carried some risk of harm'.

Gross negligence manslaughter was reintroduced into English law by the House of Lords in *R* v *Adomako* (1994). The decision was in line with the actions of the Court of Appeal decision in *R* v *Prentice* (1994). The mens rea for the offence was gross negligence, which is not fully defined. Lord Mackay in *R* v *Adomako* (1994) was unwilling to provide a detailed definition of gross negligence. However, he quoted Lord Hewart CJ, who in *R* v *Bateman* (1925) stated that it was 'such disregard for the life and safety of others as to amount to a crime against the State and conduct deserving punishment'.

The problem with this definition is that it is far too broad. No guidance is given on whether an objective or subjective test should be applied. In *R v Prentice* (1994), Lord Taylor CJ identified four variations of gross negligence, two being objective and two being subjective. The subjective options he stated as 'actual foresight of the risk coupled with determination nevertheless to run it', and 'an appreciation of the risk coupled with an intention to avoid it'. The objective options he stated as 'indifference to an obvious risk of injury to health' and 'inattention or failure to advert to a serious risk'.

Subsequent judgements, while attempting to clarify the definition, appear to have broadened it still further. In *R v Singh* (1999), the Court of Appeal took an objective approach and approved the direction of the trial judge who stated that '...the circumstances must be such that a reasonably prudent person would have foreseen a serious and obvious risk of death.' However, in *R v Lidar* (1999), the Court of Appeal stated that gross negligence could be objective or subjective. In A–G's Reference (No 2 of 1999), the Court of Appeal stated that it was not always necessary to consider the mental state of the defendant at all, because, in some situations, actions alone may justify the imposition of criminal liability. Following these cases, it would appear that gross negligence can now be defined in terms of subjective or objective criteria, and may be applied in respect of the physical conduct or mental state of the defendant.

We are thus left with a position where both types of involuntary manslaughter have significant objective elements, and thus seem to be out of step with most other important areas of criminal law.

Non-fatal offences

The operation of fault in non-fatal offences is also inconsistent. It is clear that all of the offences require proof of fault for a conviction. However, while some of the offences have a *mens rea* requirement which equates with the harm caused, others do not.

According to s.18 of the **Offences Against the Person Act 1861**, assault and battery require intention or subjective recklessness to bring about the prohibited result of the *actus reus*. However, sections 47 and 20 both require intention or recklessness to bring about a result less serious than that specified in the *actus reus*. If charged with a s.47 offence, the accused can be found guilty of causing actual bodily harm, despite only having the intention of, or knowingly taking the risk of, frightening or unlawfully touching the victim. Under s.20, a conviction can be sustained for wounding or causing grievous bodily harm when the accused only intended or took the risk of causing some harm. It would appear that under sections 47 and 20, the accused is held legally responsible for a level of harm higher than that he or she is at fault in bringing about. He or she may have voluntarily done the act which caused the consequences, but did not intend or knowingly take the risk of the consequences being so serious.

The distinction between legal fault and motive

In criminal law, the legal fault requirement is stipulated in the definition of the offences. However, criminal law takes no account of motive. This is illustrated clearly by the issue of mercy killings. People who perpetrate mercy killings do so out of care for the victim and often with the best possible motive, but they will still be technically guilty of murder.

In *R* v *Cox* (1992), Dr Cox was found guilty of attempted murder. He had injected a terminally-ill, elderly patient, who was suffering constant severe pain, with a lethal drug, after the patient asked him to end her suffering. Where possible, the judge may take account of motive when sentencing, and Dr Cox was given a suspended prison sentence.

In *ex parte Dianne Pretty* (2001) the House of Lords held that the husband of a motor neurone disease sufferer could be subject to a criminal prosecution if he helped his wife end her life. Consequently, Dianne Pretty was forced to endure a slower and more painful death than would have been necessary had she won her case.

Strict liability offences

There are many crimes for which there is no fault requirement in terms of *mens rea*. This is a significant departure from the principle that to be guilty of a criminal offence a defendant should be proved to be at fault.

Strict liability offences are generally regulatory offences, concerned with public safety, and usually made by statute. They cover situations such as minor road traffic offences, food safety laws, protection of the environment, and the sale of alcohol and tobacco to under-age children.

In *Smedleys* v *Breed* (1974), a caterpillar was found in a tin of peas. The defendants were convicted under s.2 of the **Food and Drugs Act 1955**, despite having taken all reasonable precautions to prevent this sort of contamination occurring. Another example is *Harrow LBC* v *Shah* in which the defendant, a newsagent, was convicted of selling a lottery ticket to a 13-year-old. The fact that he had told staff not to sell lottery tickets to under 16s, had put up a notice in the shop to this effect, and had told staff to ask for proof of identity was irrelevant.

The courts are reluctant, in the absence of express statutory permission, to impose strict liability for offences which are truly criminal in nature. In such situations there is a presumption that *mens rea* is required. In *Sweet* v *Parsley* (1970), the defendant owned a house which she rented to students. Unknown to her, they smoked cannabis on the premises. She was charged with being concerned in the management of premises used for the purpose of smoking cannabis. On appeal, her conviction was quashed on the basis that the offence was truly criminal and carried a serious social stigma. This principle was adopted in the more recent case of *B* v *DPP* (2000). In this case, a 15-year-old boy encouraged a 13-year-old girl (she claimed to be over 14) to have oral sex with him. He was convicted of committing an act of gross indecency on a child under the age of 14. Both the trial judge and the Court of Appeal agreed that the offence was one of strict liability. However, the House of Lords quashed the conviction on the basis that *mens rea* was required because the offence was truly criminal in nature and carried a serious social stigma. The case of *R* v *Prince* (1874), in which the defendant was convicted of abducting a girl under the age of 16 (she was 13 but claimed to be 18) is outdated and no longer applicable.

While strict liability offences do not require *mens rea*, they do require an *actus reus*. The *actus reus* must be committed voluntarily, so it would appear that even strict liability offences are dependent on proof of fault, albeit to a lesser extent.

Absolute liability offences

Absolute liability offences are those which do not require *mens rea* and do not require the act to be carried out voluntarily. These types of offences are sometimes referred to as 'state of affairs' offences.

In *Winzar* v *Chief Constable of Kent* (1983), the accused was charged with being found drunk on the highway. He had entered a hospital while drunk and had been asked to leave. When he refused, the police were called. The police forcefully removed him from the hospital to their car, which was parked on the highway. He was convicted, despite having been forced by the police to commit the offence.

Mandatory sentences

Mandatory sentences for murder under the **Crime (Sentencing) Act 1997** would also appear to go against the principle that decisions in criminal law should be based on the amount of fault displayed by the defendant. The mandatory life sentence for murder has been widely criticised, particularly in the context of 'mercy killing' cases such as *R* v *Cox* (1992). The 1997 Act has been challenged under the **Human Rights Act 1998**. It imposes automatic sentences for subsequent offences, such as a second serious sexual or violent assault, or a third drug trafficking offence or domestic burglary. These automatic sentences can only be avoided in 'exceptional' circumstances. In *R* v *Offen* (2001), in order to prevent a possible breach of Articles 3 or 5, the Court of Appeal interpreted 'exceptional' to mean any case where there was not a danger to the public, thus significantly weakening the scope of the Act to impose automatic sentences for subsequent offences.

The criticism of mandatory sentences is based on the fact that they allow no flexibility and do not allow fault to be taken into account. In 1989, a House of Lords select committee recommended that the mandatory life sentence for murder be abolished. The decision in *R* v *Offen* suggests that the principle should be limited to cases where there is a danger to the public.

Fault in the law of tort

Negligence

For a claimant to succeed in an action of negligence, three elements must be proved: duty of care, breach and causation. In deciding whether there has been a breach of duty the courts will apply the standard of the 'reasonable man'. This considers whether the 'reasonable man' would have behaved as the defendant did.

In *Bolton* v *Stone* (1951), the claimant had been hit by a cricket ball. The court considered the likelihood of the risk of injury to be very small on the basis that balls had flown out of the cricket ground between six and ten times in 30 years. Furthermore, the defendants had already erected a tall fence around the ground. In the circumstances, the court was of the view that the 'reasonable man' would have acted the same way and would not have taken further preventative measures.

In *Paris* v *Stepney LBC* (1951), however, the court held the defendants to be in breach of duty. The defendants did not provide a welder, who only had one eye, with goggles. Sparks flew into his good eye. The court held the defendants to be in breach of duty because the severity of the potential damage was very high and the cost of eliminating the risk, i.e. of providing the goggles, was very low. In the circumstances, the 'reasonable man' would have provided the claimant with goggles.

Occupiers' liability

Occupiers' liability is also based on the notion of reasonableness. The **Occupiers' Liability Acts 1957** and **1984** make occupiers responsible for the safety of visitors and non-visitors respectively while on their premises. An occupier fulfils the duty owed by taking reasonable precautions. In *Martin* v *Middlesbrough Corporation* (1965), the council was held liable to the child claimant who slipped in a playground and cut herself on a broken glass bottle. The council did not have adequate arrangements in place for the disposal of such litter. However, in *Sawyer* v *Simonds* (1966), the defendants were not liable when a customer fell and injured himself on broken glass while in their pub. They had made arrangements for the bar to be checked every 20 minutes and this was considered by the court to be reasonable.

Under s.2(2)(b), people on the premises in the exercise of their calling are owed a lower duty of care, since they are expected to know what they are doing. There is a shift in responsibility from the occupier to the visitor. In *Roles* v *Nathan* (1963), chimney sweeps had been hired to clean central heating flues. They were warned of danger from fumes but entered the chimney and died. The occupiers were not liable since they were not at fault. The sweeps were acting in the exercise of their calling, so it was their responsibility to know about the dangers.

Fault of the victim: contributory negligence

In apportioning damages in tort, the law takes into account the fault of the victim. Section 1(1) of the **Law Reform (Contributory Negligence) Act 1945** states that where any person suffers damage as the result partly of his own fault, the damages recoverable shall be reduced to such an extent as the court thinks just and equitable, having regard to the claimant's share in the responsibility for the damage.

In *Froom* v *Butcher* (1975), the claimant's damages were reduced by 25%. He had been involved in a vehicle accident caused by the negligence of the defendant, but was partly responsible for his injuries, as he had not been wearing a seat belt.

Nuisance

While it can be seen that liability in negligence or occupiers' liability depends upon proof of fault, in other areas of the law of tort this is not the case.

Nuisance involves strict liability since it does not matter if the defendant took reasonable care to avoid the nuisance. Reasonableness in nuisance is concerned with the level of interference with the claimant's enjoyment of his or her land. However, motive or malice of the defendant is an issue. This is illustrated by *Christie* v *Davy* (1893). Whenever the claimant gave music lessons, the defendant deliberately shrieked and banged on the adjoining wall. The claimant succeeded because the defendant had acted maliciously.

Rylands v *Fletcher* (1868)

The rule in *Rylands* v *Fletcher* originally involved strict liability for damage caused by something escaping from the defendant's land. This rule only applied to non-natural or artificial use of land. In this case, the defendants were liable for escape of water into a mine, even though there was no wrongful intent or negligence. The water constituted a non-natural use, due to the non-natural quantity. However, the case of *Cambridge Water Company* v *Eastern Counties Leather plc* (1994) introduced a negligence requirement. The House of Lords held that under the rule, defendants would only be liable for damage of a foreseeable type.

Vicarious liability

Under the principle of vicarious liability, liability is imposed for someone else's fault. A key area in which the principle operates is employment. Employers are held vicariously liable for torts committed by their employees in the course of their employment. No liability will be incurred for acts done which are considered to be outside the course of employment or when the employee is considered to be 'on a frolic of his own'. The principle applies in respect of prohibited acts, and acts which are carried out in a prohibited or unauthorised manner. This is shown by *Rose* v *Plenty* (1976). The claimant, aged 13, was helping the defendant deliver milk. This was forbidden by his employers. The claimant was injured through the defendant's employee's negligent driving. The employers were held liable. The employee was doing what he was employed to do, i.e. deliver milk, but he was doing it in an unauthorised manner. While it may appear unfair on the employer, the principle of vicarious liability is justified on the basis that the act is done for the employer's benefit, and the victim is more likely to be compensated due to the requirement of compulsory insurance.

Liability for defective products

Liability for defective products was dependent upon proof of fault until the **Consumer Protection Act 1987** was introduced. Claimants had to prove that the manufacturer was in breach of his or her duty of care. The 1987 Act imposed what is, in effect, strict liability on producers for damage caused by defective products.

Moves towards a no-fault based system for accident victims

In more recent years, there has been a move from the laissez-faire ideal which dominated in the nineteenth century. The law has increasingly come to focus on the injured victim rather than the blameworthy individual. Twentieth-century legislation provides a partial no-fault based system.

The Welfare State legislation created the Department of Social Security. Victims of accidents at work are now able to claim compensation from the state, without the need to prove negligence. Social security benefits are also available to those who suffer illness or disability.

Fault in the law of contract

The basis of contract law is that parties have entered into a legally binding agreement and that a party that does not perform what was promised is at fault and liable to compensate the other parties.

The doctrine of frustration

If no one is at fault, then under the general principle of no liability without fault, no one should be liable. This is evident in the doctrine of frustration.

Frustration arises when an event occurs over which the parties have no control and which makes performance of the contract impossible. In *Taylor* v *Caldwell* (1863), a hall was hired with the purpose that it be used for a concert. The hall burned down beforehand. Since the hall was the subject matter of the contract, and had clearly been destroyed, performance of the contract was impossible. However, a contract will not be frustrated if it merely becomes more difficult to perform, as illustrated by *Davis Contractors Ltd* v *Fareham UDC* (1956). In this case, it was unsuccessfully argued that the contract was frustrated due to escalating costs.

The common law position in the event of frustration used to be that gains and losses lay where they fell. This could be unfair, and sometimes result in one party bearing all the losses suffered. The situation was improved by the **Law Reform (Frustrated Contracts) Act 1943**, which regulates the financial position between parties when the contract is frustrated and provides for loss to be apportioned more fairly.

Misrepresentation

Misrepresentation may be defined as an untrue statement of fact made by one party to the contract to the other, which induces the latter to enter into the contract. In *Smith* v *Land & House Property Corporation* (1884), the landlord of a property being sold described the sitting occupier as a desirable tenant, in the knowledge that the person in question was not good at paying rent. This was fraudulent misrepresentation; the landlord was at fault and was liable in misrepresentation to the purchaser.

Innocent misrepresentation is an exception to the principle of no liability without proof of fault. The maker of the innocent statement is not blameworthy for the statement, yet will still be held liable.

By examining the doctrine of frustration and the law of misrepresentation it can be seen that in contract law, liability is, for the most part, dependent upon proof of fault.

Should liability in criminal law depend upon proof of fault?

Tip

Candidates may be required to consider whether liability should depend on proof of fault. Arguments about strict liability are relevant, but it is important to consider too why liability should depend on proof of fault, and the problems that the principle of no liability with proof of fault presents.

The effect of criminal sanctions and procedures

Criminal law is enforced through state procedures and sanctions, focused on the defendant. A guilty verdict will result in the imposition of a sentence on the defendant. The court has a wide range of sentences at its disposal, some of which will directly limit the liberty of the convict, such as electronic tagging, probation and incarceration.

Punishment, however, is only justified if people are at fault. Depriving people of their liberty or imposing other punishments are serious infringements of personal freedom. Furthermore, the liberty of the convicted individual will also be affected by his or her criminal record, which may, for example, prevent access to certain jobs and thus adversely affect opportunities. Opportunities in turn will be affected by the public condemnation of the individual's offence(s). Minor road traffic offences, which are strict liability, do not result in a criminal record, but there is still a stigma attached to strict liability offences, e.g. the butcher who unknowingly sells bad meat.

It is because of these issues that the legal profession, the judges and the legislature regard the principle of no liability without proof of fault as being so important in criminal law.

Strict liability offences

Despite proof of fault being regarded as so important in criminal law, it must be noted that there are some strict liability offences, which do not require *mens rea*.

Such offences typically deal with issues such as public health and safety, protection of the environment and road traffic. There is the further advantage that court time is saved and consequently costs are reduced when there is no need to prove *mens rea*.

In the case of *Gammon (Hong Kong) Ltd* v *Attorney General* (1984), the privy council said that if the prosecution had to prove *mens rea* in even the smallest regulatory offence, the administration of justice might very quickly come to a complete standstill. Court time is saved, as people are more likely to plead guilty. Those in favour of strict liability offences argue that higher standards of care are encouraged. Social scientist Barbara Wootten has defended strict liability, suggesting that if the objective of the criminal law is to prevent socially damaging activities, it would be absurd to turn a blind eye to those who cause harm because of carelessness, negligence or even by accident. There is also the fact that strict liability offences carry relatively low sentences in recognition of the lower levels of culpability.

However, those who argue against strict liability suggest that there is no real evidence that it increases levels of care. This may be partly attributable to the lack of incentive to act reasonably if no account is taken of attempts to prevent the prohibited act occurring. People are also more likely to accept their guilt and punishment if fault has to be proved. In Australia, a defence of all due care is available. Were this defence available in England, it would deal with situations where defendants, such as Mr Shah (in *Harrow LBC* v *Shah*), take all reasonable care to avoid committing the offence.

Finally, the argument that in strict liability offences the penalty is small is equally dubious. It is inconsistent with justice to convict someone who is not guilty in the normal sense of the word just because the penalty is small.

Should liability in civil law depend on proof of fault?

In civil law, compensation is regarded as the responsibility of those at fault

Civil law, like criminal law, is based on the notion of individual responsibility. Individuals choose to behave the way they do and should therefore accept responsibility for the outcomes of their actions. Individuals can choose to be more careful so as to minimise the harm they cause. It is not right that individuals who have made the choice to exercise more care should pay for the harm caused by those who have not. However, it is unfair to punish an individual for harm caused by accident, because being more careful would not have prevented the harm and it was not possible for the blameless individual to be more careful.

Gradual move towards a no-fault based system for accident victims

The advantage of the system of no fault liability for accident victims is that those who are entitled to compensation or social security are more likely to receive it than they would be to receive compensation under the fault-based tort system. It may be fairer for more people to receive compensation, albeit lesser in amount. However, there is the perception of unfairness in that all of society has to pay for what often amounts to the acts of blameworthy individuals.

The Consumer Protection Act 1987

The **Consumer Protection Act 1987** imposes strict liability on producers for damage caused by defective products. However, while it is the producer who directly provides the compensation to the claimant, the burden is indirectly borne by society, because as the risk of liability increases, so too will insurance premiums, and this cost will be passed on to consumers.

Insurance premiums

While some victims are able to claim compensation without the need to prove fault, there are many who are still required to do so. Road accident victims and victims of medical errors have to satisfy the negligence requirements, despite the defendants being insured. In fact, it may partly be the insurance issue that prevents the extension of the no-fault system. Insurance premiums would inevitably have to rise and might become unaffordable. More people would risk driving without insurance and medical practitioners would be less willing to provide anything other than treatment that they considered totally safe.

Contract law

In contract law, the rules on frustration of contract and innocent misrepresentation do impose liabilities on innocent parties. The **Law Reform (Frustrated Contracts Act) 1943** operates in a fair and straightforward manner and has resulted in very little litigation. The rules on innocent misrepresentation are more contentious, but arguably it is right that a party that volunteers information, on the basis of which the other party acts, should ultimately be responsible for the accuracy of that information.

Conclusion

It would seem that the imposition of liability without fault is more acceptable in civil law than in criminal law. The unfairness of leaving an injured victim without compensation increasingly outweighs the unfairness of blameless individuals being required to provide that compensation indirectly through state funds or insurance.

Despite the arguments against the imposition of strict liability in tort, including the doubt that it raises safety standards, there are areas in which there is no need to prove fault, such as nuisance, *Rylands* v *Fletcher* and under the principle of vicarious liability.

In criminal law, however, the desire to protect the blameless individual from the outcomes of state procedures and sanctions makes imposition of liability without fault less acceptable. Strict liability offences can only be created by the legislature in limited circumstances.

> **Tip**
>
> Most exam questions require candidates to consider the *extent* to which liability in English law depends upon proof of fault, or *how far* liability in English law depends upon proof of fault. This can be done by explaining and illustrating with material drawn from the specification the general principle of English law that liability does depend upon proof of fault, and then taking the same approach with the exceptions to the general principle. Better candidates will draw on material from a wide range of laws within the criminal and civil law. While many candidates are able to give a broad account of the role of fault in criminal law, relatively few candidates venture far beyond negligence when considering the civil law. Stronger candidates are able to use a wider range of torts, including occupiers' liability, nuisance, *Rylands* v *Fletcher* and the principle of vicarious liability.

Judicial creativity

> **Tip**
>
> It is important to be able to address the extent to which judges are able to display creativity in the operation of the system of judicial precedent. Some mechanisms of precedent aid judicial creativity and some impede it, and in some areas of law, these mechanisms have been operational in either developing or restricting the development of the law.

Characteristics of the doctrine of precedent which limit judicial creativity

Requirement to follow previous decisions

The doctrine of precedent is based on the idea of *stare decisis*, which means to stand by what has been decided. The courts are bound to follow the decisions made in earlier cases. The doctrine of precedent operates within a hierarchical court structure, with the lower courts being bound by the precedents made in the higher courts. The binding part of the judgement is called the *ratio decidendi*, meaning the legal reason for the decision. Other things said in the judgement which are not part of the reasons for the decision are referred to as *obiter dicta*.

Judges are dependent on cases being brought before the courts

Judges are dependent on cases being brought before them in the higher courts for the opportunity to create law. For example, judges had felt since the 1960s that the old rule of a builder not owing a duty in tort to the person to whom he sold a property was unfair. In *Dutton* v *Bognor Regis UDC* (1972), Lord Denning said *in obiter* that the builder should owe a duty of care, but the opportunity to follow this persuasive precedent did not arise until 1978 in *Batty* v *Metropolitan Property Realisations Ltd*.

Characteristics of the doctrine of precedent which aid judicial creativity

Practice Statement

Under the 1966 Practice Statement, the House of Lords has the power to depart from its previous decisions when it appears 'right to do so'. The Law Lords have used this power sparingly because of an overall desire to achieve certainty in the law.

However, despite the limitations set out in the Practice Statement and the self-imposed restraint which has characterised the Law Lords in a majority of cases heard since 1966, it has been used to bring about significant changes in the law. Notable examples are that occupiers have some duty in respect of trespassers, *Herrington* v *British Railways Board* (1972), that no participant can use duress as a defence to a murder charge, *R* v *Howe* (1987), that *Hansard* can in certain circumstances be referred to when interpreting a statute, *Pepper* v *Hart* (1993), and most recently in the case of *R* v *G* (2004), that the *mens rea* of recklessness should always be subjective, overruling *R* v *Caldwell* (1982).

Overruling

Higher courts can always overrule earlier precedents set in lower courts. Overruling must not be confused with reversing, which involves a higher court changing the outcome of a case on appeal.

Distinguishing

Judges in all courts may avoid following a precedent by finding that the facts of the case before them are materially different from those of the case in which the binding precedent was set. In *Balfour* v *Balfour* (1919), Mrs Balfour was unable to enforce a maintenance agreement made with her husband. The *ratio decidendi* of the case was that there is no intention to create legal relations when agreements are made within marriage. In *Merritt* v *Merritt* (1970), the defendant husband sought to rely on the Balfour principle to avoid honouring an agreement he had made with his estranged wife. The court distinguished the case on the material difference that the agreement, albeit made within marriage, had been made after the couple had separated, and the husband had to transfer the house to the wife as agreed. The decision limited the scope of the Balfour principle and created a new rule in respect of separated couples.

Dissenting judgements

Judges in the higher courts may disagree with the legal principles being applied in cases before them. In such cases, they may deliver a dissenting judgement, in which they outline principles they believe should apply. Dissenting judgements are persuasive precedents and so may be followed in future cases. Some key areas of law have developed from such judgements. The law on negligent misstatement was developed from the dissenting judgement of Lord Denning in *Candler* v *Crane Christmas* (1951). The majority judges held that accountants, who prepared a company's accounts, knowing that they would be relied upon by third parties, owed no duty of care. Lord Denning, however, stipulated the circumstances in which such a duty should be owed. His judgement formed the basis of the decision in *Hedley Byrne* v *Heller* (1964), in which it was held that, had there not been a disclaimer, the claimants could have recovered compensation caused by the negligent misstatement. The circumstances outlined in *Caparo* v *Dickman* (1991) for when such a duty should be owed are very similar to those originally outlined by Lord Denning.

Obiter dicta statements

When delivering their judgements, judges sometimes speculate on what their decision would have been had the facts been slightly different. These *obiter* statements are persuasive and may become the *ratio decidendi* of future cases. In *R* v *Brown* (1993) the defendants, who had engaged in sadomasochistic activities, were unable to rely on the defence of consent when prosecuted under the **Offences Against the Person Act 1861**. However, the Lords stated *in obiter* that consent could be a defence to painful practices such as tattooing and piercing. In *R* v *Wilson* (1996), the defendant husband was able to rely on this defence when he used a hot knife to brand his initials onto his wife's buttocks at her request. The Court of Appeal held that the defendant was engaged in body decoration, which was similar to body piercing or tattooing.

Other examples include *R* v *R* (1991), where the House of Lords was influenced by Court of Appeal arguments on the issue of rape within marriage, and *Overseas Tankship (UK) Ltd.* v *Mort's Dock & Engineering Co. Ltd.* (*The Wagon Mound No 1*) (1961) where a decision of the Judicial Committee of the Privy Council on remoteness of damage was followed in the English courts.

The Court of Appeal

In practice, the Court of Appeal makes a great deal of new law. A good example is *R* v *Nedrick* (1986), which clarified the law on oblique intent and has become the leading judgement, despite several earlier House of Lords decisions. It was also the Court of Appeal in *R* v *Prentice* (1994) that effectively reintroduced gross negligence manslaughter into the modern law. However, the Court of Appeal does not have the power to overrule its earlier decisions, despite Lord Denning's efforts in *Davis* v *Johnson* (1979) to secure the same powers for the Court as those enjoyed by the House of Lords under the Practice Statement.

Evidence of the ability of judges to be creative and develop the law, despite the constraints of precedent, is provided by the fact that in a number of significant areas of law, almost all the rules are judge-made. This presents an opportunity to refer to areas of substantive law in detail. For example, in criminal law, the rules on the mens rea of murder, on involuntary manslaughter and on defences such as intoxication and self-defence may be considered. In tort, reference can be made to areas such as the development of the rules relating to nervous shock or economic loss, private nuisance and the rule in *Rylands* v *Fletcher*. In contract law, the rules on formation and discharge of contracts are obvious examples.

The extent to which judges can display creativity in statutory interpretation

The literal rule

In theory, judges should have little opportunity for creativity because their task is to apply statutes as they are written. Supporters of the literal rule argue that judges should do this in all circumstances. Judges who follow the literal rule are not creative and do not develop the law, even when common sense demands it. An example is *Fisher* v *Bell* (1961). A shopkeeper was charged under the **Offensive Weapons Act 1959** for offering for sale an offensive weapon. He had displayed flick knives in the shop window. The court held that no offence had been committed as, according to contract law, what he had done amounted to an invitation to treat and not to an offer.

The mischief rule

When interpreting a statute, judges may be creative in that they broaden or narrow its application. This is particularly relevant in terms of the mischief and purposive approaches. The mischief rule requires judges to look back to the law before the Act in question was made in order to determine the gap in the law that the Act was intended to remedy. In *Smith* v *Hughes* (1960), a prostitute was prosecuted under **The Street Offences Act 1958**, under which it was an offence to solicit in the street. In this case, the prostitute had attracted the attention of men who were in the street by tapping on her first floor window. The court held, using the mischief approach, that the mischief the Act had been passed to prevent was men in the street being accosted by prostitutes, and that therefore she was guilty. The Act was thus made broader in application because it was not limited to situations where the prostitute was in the street itself.

A further example is *The Royal College of Nursing* v *DHSS* (1981), in which the House of Lords had to decide how the **Abortion Act 1967** should be interpreted. The Act stated that lawful abortion requires that a pregnancy 'is terminated by a registered medical practitioner'. In 1967, the method of producing an abortion was surgical and so would have needed to be performed by a doctor. However, by the 1980s abortions were being induced by drip feeding a drug which caused the fetus to be discharged from the uterus. This was performed by midwives and nurses. The House of Lords held that the mischief the Act had been passed to prevent was illegal, backstreet abortion, and that therefore it was legal for midwives and nurses to administer the drug.

The purposive approach

The purposive approach to legislation has become increasingly popular among English judges, particularly since the UK joined the European Union, because in many countries the law is stated in general principles which can be applied to a broad range of circumstances. EU law is drafted in such terms and it is important that English judges take a purposive approach to interpreting Acts of Parliament which have been passed to comply with European obligations.

Lord Denning, in *Bulmer* v *Bollinger* (1974), pointed out that when interpreting such legislation, English courts must depart from the traditional methods of interpreting domestic statutes and follow the European pattern: 'No longer must they examine words in meticulous detail. No longer must they argue about the precise grammatical sense. They must look to the purpose or intent.'

The European Convention on Human Rights is similarly set out in broad terms. The judges in the European Court of Human Rights therefore also use the purposive approach. The **Human Rights Act 1998** requires that all legislation be interpreted so that, as far as possible, it is compatible with the convention. This will inevitably result in English judges increasingly using the purposive approach.

Following the House of Lords decision in *Pepper* v *Hart* (1993), judges may now make reference to *Hansard* in limited circumstances, as an aid to interpretation. It is arguable that this decision was brought about by the shift in favour from the literal to the purposive approach that has occurred in recent years.

The balance between the roles of Parliament and the judiciary

The constitutional position

Constitutionally, it is the role of Parliament to create law and, as Lord Radcliffe said, 'it is unacceptable constitutionally that there should be two sources of law-making at work at the same time'. The basis of the constitutional position is that Parliament is democratically elected (at least, the House of Commons is) and that the legislative programme will to some extent be influenced by the electorate. Judges, on the other hand, are not elected and are arguably not representative of the population they serve.

The constitutional role of judges has changed in recent years through the UK's membership of the European Union. Section 2(4) of the **European Communities Act 1972** states that European Community law should take precedence over English law. In giving effect to this section, English judges have been able to exercise powers that were not available to them in the past. For example, in *R* v *Secretary of State for Transport ex parte Factortame* (1990), the European Court of Justice held that domestic courts are entitled to ignore provisions of domestic legislation which are in conflict with provisions of directly enforceable European law. In this case it was also held that domestic courts could suspend domestic legislation while awaiting a decision of the European Court of Justice.

The **Human Rights Act 1998** has also significantly altered the balance between the judges and Parliament. Section 3 requires legislation to be interpreted so that, as far as possible, it is compatible with the European Convention on Human Rights. This was most dramatically demonstrated in *A and others* v *Secretary of State for the Home Department* (2004). The House of Lords held that s.23 of the **Anti-terrorism, Crime and Security Act 2001**, in permitting the detention of suspected international terrorists indefinitely without charge or trial, was incompatible with Articles 5 and 14 of the European Convention on Human Rights.

Policy

Formulation of policy is the role of Parliament. Policy is a set of ideas about what should be done and sets out objectives and intended directions of change. Ronald Dworkin made a distinction between rules and principles on the one hand and policies on the other. A policy, he said, is a standard setting out of a goal to be achieved, usually in terms of the economic, social or political well-being of the community. A principle, on the other hand, sets individual rights above communal well-being and imposes a standard of justice or fairness or some other moral dimension. Matters of policy should be left to the elected legislators; judges should concern themselves only with legal principles.

On the whole, judges tend to agree with this view, at least in what they say. However, judges are sometimes placed in positions where they have to make policy decisions. First, judges have a role in judicial review and as guardians of individual rights. By giving priority to individual rights over policy, and thereby ruling against the government, they will be making decisions which could be seen as being political and which have an impact on policy goals. For example, the House of Lords decision in *A and others* v *Secretary of State for the Home Department* (December 2004) that detention of suspected international terrorists without trial or charge is unlawful, will inevitably impact to some extent on how the government deals with terrorism in the future.

The second problem for judges is that they sometimes have to make controversial decisions, which will inevitably have policy implications. In *Gillick* v *West Norfolk and Wisbech Area Health Authority* (1985), the issue for the judges to decide was whether or not girls under the age of 16 should be prescribed contraceptives without parental consent. There was no consensus on the issue and Parliament had given no guidance. The House of Lords held that a girl under 16 could be prescribed contraceptives without parental consent only if she fully understood the issues involved. This case created the 'Gillick competent child'. There have been similar issues raised more recently with girls under 16 having abortions without parental consent.

Policy in statutory interpretation

Judges who argued for the literal rule usually justified it on the grounds that it was based on the principle that they should not change the wording of statutes, because to do so would be to usurp the legislative function and that was not their role. If the outcome of a judicial decision were inconvenient, the proper solution would be for Parliament to make any alteration it felt to be necessary.

Judges adopted this approach in *In the Estate of Bravda* (1968), where the Court of Appeal had to deal with an unfortunate situation under the **Wills Act 1837**. The Act clearly stated that any beneficiary who signed a will automatically lost his or her right to benefit under the will. In this case, a man's daughters were the main beneficiaries, and the Court felt that it would be right to ensure that where there are two independent witnesses, the mere fact that a beneficiary has signed as a witness should not operate (as it then did) to defeat the intentions of the testator. However, rather than adopt either the golden or mischief rule and change the wording of the Act, the Court felt that, as a policy issue, the change should be made by Parliament. **The Wills Acts 1968** was passed to make the necessary changes.

On the other hand, there are examples of decisions in statutory interpretation which are based on policy. In *Re Sigsworth* (1935), the Court ruled that a man who murdered his mother, who had died intestate, should not benefit from his crime. It was contrary to public policy to allow such an undesirable outcome. The golden rule was used and the words of the statute amended.

In the case of *The Royal College of Nursing* v *DHSS* (1981), the majority in the House of Lords was influenced by what it considered to be the policy of the **Abortion Act 1967**, namely broadening of the grounds of lawful abortion and ensuring that it was carried out with proper skill. The two dissenting judges, Lords Wilberforce and Edmund-Davies, argued that the Act should not be rewritten because it dealt with 'a controversial subject involving moral or social judgements on which opinions strongly differ'. In other words, this was a policy issue, which should be left to Parliament.

Professor Griffith has argued that where there is ambiguity in a statute, the judges choose the interpretation which best suits their view of what policy should be. The example that best fits this argument is *Bromley London Borough Council* v *Greater London*

Council (1983). Griffith claimed that what the House of Lords was doing in this case was making a choice between two interpretations, based not on what Parliament intended, but primarily on 'the Law Lords' strong preference for the principles of the market economy with a dislike of heavy subsidisation for social purposes'.

Policy in criminal law

Intoxication

In *DPP* v *Majewski* (1977), policy issues were clearly the basis of the decision. Majewski, after drinking alcohol and taking drugs over a period of 24 hours, attacked people in a public house and then the police officers who tried to arrest him. The House of Lords refused to accept the defence of intoxication on policy grounds — it is a prime purpose of the law to protect people from violence and to allow intoxication as a defence would leave the citizen unprotected from such violence. Lord Salmon said: 'If there were to be no penal sanction for any injury unlawfully inflicted under the complete mastery of drink or drugs, voluntarily taken, the social consequences would be appalling.'

Provocation

In *R* v *Ahluwalia* (1992), where the defendant had clearly not acted in the heat of the moment, it was held that important considerations of public policy would be involved should provocation be redefined so as possibly to blur the distinction between sudden loss of self-control and deliberate retribution. The court was not willing to consider such a change.

Consent to the infliction of violence

It has long been recognised that to take part in sporting activities is to consent to the possible infliction of some degree of injury. In the case of boxing, for example, some injury is almost inevitable. In *R* v *Wilson* (1996), there is the acceptance that within marriage, consent can be given to the infliction of injury, yet in *R* v *Brown and others* (1994), consenting adults were found guilty. Reading the judgements of the House of Lords, it is clear that they were using policy considerations. For example, Lord Templeman expressed the view that 'society was entitled to protect itself against a cult of violence. Pleasure derived from the infliction of pain was an evil thing. Cruelty was uncivilised'.

Policy in tort

The extension of negligence into ever more diverse areas has also led to policy issues being raised with reference to wider social or economic considerations rather than to precedent or to legal principles to justify decisions. This is apparent in the law relating to pure economic loss. In *Spartan Steel and Alloys Ltd* v *Martin & Co (Contractors) Ltd* (1972), Lord Denning openly based his leading judgement on policy. He said: 'At bottom I think the question of recovering economic loss is one of policy. Whenever the courts draw a line to mark out the bounds of duty, they do it as a matter of policy so as to limit the responsibility of the defendant. Whenever the courts set bounds to the damages recoverable — saying that they are, or are not, too remote — they do it as a matter of policy so as to limit the liability of the defendant.'

A similar situation can be observed in the development of the law relating to nervous shock. In *Alcock* v *Chief Constable of South Yorkshire* (1992), the House of Lords, influenced by the floodgates argument, set out the criteria which successful secondary victims have to fulfil. Lord Oliver openly used the word 'policy' in explaining his decision to limit the range of potential victims to whom a duty of care could be owed.

Should judges create law?

Tip

An exam question may ask whether judges should make law. This requires consideration of the benefits and the problems posed by judicial law making. It is also useful to consider the views of the judges themselves. Stronger candidates will be able to draw on a wide range of arguments and provide illustration.

Benefits of judicial law-making

Flexibility

One of the advantages of the common law system is that the law is able to respond to new situations. Within the limits set by precedent and the rules of statutory interpretation, judges are able to develop the law in ways that reflect changing social and technological circumstances. For example, the law has been adapted to deal with the effect of life support systems on the exact point of death, *R* v *Malcherek and Steel* (1981), and technical developments in the way abortions are carried out, *The Royal College of Nursing* v *DHSS* (1981).

In contract law, the postal rule has been adapted to deal with instantaneous forms of communication, *Entores* v *Miles Far East Corpn* (1955).

It takes many months for an Act of Parliament to be passed. However, the courts may respond immediately to a novel situation. In *McLoughlin* v *O'Brian* (1983), the House of Lords extended the law on nervous shock to cover situations where the secondary victim came upon the 'immediate aftermath'.

Insufficient parliamentary time

The government will be intent on pushing through a legislative program which fulfils its political goals. Furthermore, in contrast to judges who have only one case before them at any one time, MPs and peers have many conflicting priorities to attend to, and inevitably the non-controversial, politically insignificant reforms to the law are often left aside for many years. For example, despite the work of the Law Commission, the law on non-fatal offences and corporate manslaughter remains unreformed. Similarly, moral issues are often not included in the legislative programme and the judiciary is consequently left to determine whether development of the law is required. This was clearly the case with husband rape. It had long been regarded by society as unacceptable, but successive parliaments had not found time for statutory change. The long-awaited decision was made in *R* v *R* (1991).

Law made by lawyers/experts

Judges have the further advantage over Parliament in that they are legal experts and thus better equipped to develop the law. Because they are trained to apply existing principles and relate developments to the existing law, the law is more likely to remain consistent and coherent. However, the development by judges of gross negligence manslaughter, based as it seems to be on civil law principles, has arguably not made the law of involuntary manslaughter either consistent or coherent.

Problems with judicial law-making

Constitutional position

While judicial law-making may be desirable for a number of reasons, the constitutional position is that Parliament creates law and the judges apply it. The reasons for this are that the formulation of policy is the role of a democratically elected parliament which will recognise the will of the electorate. Judges are unelected. In addition, they are arguably not representative of the population. Judges are drawn from a narrow social group and this raises the possibility, identified by Professor Griffith, that they will inevitably have views which reflect this narrow social background. Women and people from ethnic minorities are under-represented, especially amongst the senior judiciary. For example, until the appointment of Lady Hale in January 2004 there were no female Law Lords.

Lack of research

When Parliament wants to introduce a new piece of legislation, there is considerable opportunity for comprehensive research. Very often, legislation will be the result of recommendations from the Law Reform bodies, which possess the expertise to research an area thoroughly. The Law Commission is a permanent law reform body and has had considerable success in having recommendations recognised in Acts of Parliament. Examples of such legislation include the **Contract (Rights of Third Parties) Act 1999** and the **Computer Misuse Act 1990**. The Green Paper stage allows for interested parties to be consulted and the passage of the bill through Parliament will involve many debates among people who are able to research the relevant issues. Judges, however, cannot be so comprehensive in their approach. Their decisions will be based on the evidence presented to them by the parties involved in the case. They cannot consider arguments about the general social, economic or moral aspects, even though their decision, as in *Gillick* v *West Norfolk and Wisbech AHA* (1986) for example, may inevitably have implications for society generally.

Judge-made law operates retrospectively

Judge-made law applies to events which have taken place prior to its creation. This can be illustrated by *Morgans* v *Launchbury* (1973), in which the House of Lords rejected

Lord Denning's concept of the matrimonial car. The decision would have applied to accidents occurring before the judgement and therefore insurers would have had to pay out in respect of a risk which had not been taken account of when the insurance premium had been fixed.

Perhaps a more familiar example is that of *R v R* (1991), the effect of which was to turn an act, which was lawful at the time it was committed, into a serious criminal offence. Nevertheless, the decision was upheld by the European Court of Human Rights. In *SW & CR v United Kingdom*, the European Court of Human Rights held that the UK had not been in breach of Article 7 of the Convention, which states that no one should be found guilty of an offence which was not an offence at the time it was committed. The Court's reasoning was that judicial law-making was well entrenched in legal tradition and the development of the law in this case had been reasonably foreseeable.

This problem does not arise with legislation, which operates prospectively. It is usually the case that legislation comes into effect on a fixed date after the Act has received the Royal Assent, in order to allow time for people to prepare for the law change.

In some countries, including the United States, cases only apply prospectively. This concept has been considered in relation to the English legal system. In a speech in 1987, the then Lord Chancellor, Lord Mackay, discussed the possibility of allowing prospective overruling, whereby the court might uphold the existing precedent in the instant case but declare it overruled for the future. The main problem with the idea is that while most litigants are prepared to accept defeat if the judge decides the law is against them, they would find it very hard to accept that they had won their case only for future litigants, not for themselves. There would seem little point in going to court at all.

Judge-made law is incremental in nature

Judges can only make law on the facts of the case before them. They cannot lay down a comprehensive code to cover all similar situations. Some areas of law, for example negligence, might be well suited to this case-by-case approach. However, with other areas it is not helpful when one small change is made, such as the introduction of gross negligence manslaughter in *R v Prentice* (1994) and *R v Adomako* (1994), when really the whole area of involuntary manslaughter needs to be properly reformed.

Judge-made law thus develops in an unstructured, random way. It is dependent on cases being brought and then appealed through to a court sufficiently senior to make a new precedent.

Complexity/technical distinctions

One of the arguments often used against precedent as a law-making process is that judges make technical distinctions between the case they are deciding and the precedent, in order to avoid following the precedent. The result of this is that the law becomes complex and confusing, with many minor technical distinctions.

Judicial preference

Judicial views on the constitutional position

There are contrasting views among judges on the extent to which they should be making new rules of law. Lord Justice Oliver argued that for judges to develop new concepts of law would be an abandonment by the court of its proper function and an assumption by it of the mantle of legislator.

Lord Scarman, by contrast, put forward the view in *McLoughlin* v *O'Brian* (1982) that the court's proper function was to adjudicate according to principle. If principle led to results which were felt to be socially unacceptable, then Parliament could legislate to overrule them. The real risk to the common law would be if it stood still, halted by a conservative judicial approach.

Judicial law-making is more acceptable in some areas of law than others

Some judges argue that the role of the judiciary should be determined by the type of law involved. The view of Lord Reid in the 1960s was that judges should not so readily create new law in areas such as property, contract, family and criminal law, where certainty is of vital importance, but that they could have more freedom to do so in the areas of tort and public and administrative law, where the judges regard their creative role as legitimate and appropriate.

Lord Devlin argued that judges should stick to activist law making, by which he meant developing the law in line with the consensus view of society, and avoid dynamic law making, which involved creating an idea outside the consensus and effectively taking sides on controversial issues. However, judges cannot avoid making decisions in controversial cases. These might be cases which are politically sensitive, such as *Bromley London Borough Council* v *GLC* (1983) and *ex parte Pinochet* (2000), or ones which raise profound moral or social issues, for example *Gillick* v *West Norfolk & Wisbech Area Health Authority* (1986) and *Airedale NHS Trust* v *Bland* (1993).

Whatever legal theorists may argue, the fact remains that, in practice, judges have to get involved in controversial areas because such cases are brought before the courts. It is difficult to see how, in deciding any of these cases, judges could have avoided engaging in dynamic law making and offending at least one section of the community.

Personal preference

Judges adopt contrasting views on their role and it is difficult to escape the conclusion that the view they take is largely a matter of personal preference. Lord Denning, in particular, had a crusading approach to judicial law making and he was determined not to be fettered by existing legal rules. He argued that it was the duty of judges to do justice and not to follow unjust precedents or restrictive approaches to statutory interpretation. But he was firmly opposed by senior Law Lords, including Viscount Simmonds, who described his approach to statutory interpretation of 'filling in the gaps' as a 'naked usurpation of the legislative function'. David Robertson writing in 1998 concluded: 'Law in almost any case that comes before the Lords turns out to be whatever their Lordships feel it ought to be.'

Conclusion

It is evident that, in some respects, Parliament is more suited than the judiciary to develop the law. However, areas of the law which are largely judge-made seem to work just as well as those made almost exclusively by Parliament. Through the doctrine of precedent and their role in statutory interpretation, judges frequently have to develop the law by clarifying, and in some cases putting right, what is written in an Act of Parliament.

Questions
& Answers

This section of the guide provides you with five questions, which cover all of the Unit 6 areas. In this examination paper, all the questions are set as essays and they are not subdivided. There will be a choice of four questions, of which you must answer two. Candidates are required to write a continuous piece of prose. However, the questions do usually ask candidates to consider more than one aspect, and the A-grade answers should give you a clear idea of the approach and structure required.

It is important to recognise that examples and supporting evidence for questions in Unit 6 can be taken from anywhere across the whole AS and A2 specification. You will notice that some of the candidate answers in this section follow the material used in this guide quite closely, while others approach the question in a different way and use examples that are not found in the guide. It would be possible to write A-grade answers to each of the questions using entirely different material. What matters in Unit 6 answers is how the material is used and how it relates to the ideas in the question.

Each question is followed by an A-grade and a C-grade answer. The A-grade answers are very strong responses and students may be able to attain a Grade A with less material than these answers contain. You are advised to aim to achieve a high standard A-grade answer rather than aiming lower and running the risk of just missing the grade. The C-grade answers have been included to illustrate some of the common problems that result in students achieving lower marks. It is recommended that you look carefully at the comments made about these answers.

To acquire the necessary skills and become more familiar with this style of examination question, it is a good idea to practise adapting the A-grade answers for different questions. You are strongly encouraged to download past papers and mark schemes from AQA (www.aqa.org.uk) or to obtain these from your teacher.

Examiner's comments

The candidate answers are accompanied by examiner's comments, preceded by the icon 🄴. These explain the elements of the answer for which marks can be awarded and are intended to give you an insight into what examiners are looking for. For A-grade answers, these comments show why high marks would be given. The comments given for C-grade answers point out the various weaknesses, which cause marks to be lost.

Law and morals

Analyse the relationship between law and morals (30 marks)

■ ■ ■

A-grade answer

There have been many different views expressed by theorists regarding the relationship between law and morals, and these views have influenced many legal reforms. It is useful to begin with an explanation of the characteristics of, and distinctions between, legal and moral rules, before proceeding to explore areas of coincidence and areas of divergence.

Law was described by Sir John Salmond as 'the body of principles recognised and applied by the state in the administration of justice'. Breach of legal rules will result in state sanctions and procedures. In criminal law there are sanctions such as imprisonment. In civil law the wrongdoer is usually ordered to compensate the victim. Other characteristics of legal rules are that they take effect at a precise time and require compulsory compliance by all members of society. An example is the Offences Against the Person Act, which has applied to everyone since 1861.

Society's code of morality is defined by Phil Harris as a set of beliefs, values, principles and standards of behaviour. Unlike legal rules, compliance with moral rules is voluntary and enforcement is informal, usually through social or domestic pressure. Moral rules develop usually over long periods of time, as conduct becomes increasingly acceptable or unacceptable. In a pluralistic society, however, such as that in the UK, the moral duties of individuals vary. For example, while some individuals regard abortion or homosexuality as immoral, others do not.

The relationship between legal and moral rules can be described as two intersecting circles. The intersection represents the coincidence of law and morals, and the areas outside the intersection represent areas of divergence.

Long-established rules, for example those prohibiting murder or theft, can be traced back to a moral source, this being the Ten Commandments. However, there are many ways in which legal and moral rules may come to coincide.

Judicial reform of the law may be influenced by public morality. In the criminal law, the House of Lords decision in *R* v *R* (1991) was influenced by the moral rule that a husband should not force his wife to have sexual intercourse. In contract law, the equitable remedy of promissory estoppel, developed by Lord Denning in *Central London Property* v *High Trees House* (1965), was influenced by the moral rule that promises should not be broken.

Legislative reform may be also be influenced by public morality. Legislative reforms of the 1960s could be said to reflect the moral ideals of that decade. As public morality has shifted toward a greater acceptance of homosexuality, the legislature has responded. The Sexual Offences Act 1967 legalised homosexuality between consenting males over the age of 21. In 1994 the age was reduced to 18 and in December 2000 it was reduced to 16.

In turn, it can be argued that legislation is sometimes introduced with the aim of educating the public to consider certain behaviour morally wrong. An example is the discrimination legislation, which aims to educate the public not to discriminate on the basis of sex, age or disability.

While there is a considerable overlap of legal and moral rules, the pluralistic nature of society means that the coincidence is partial. Britain has a population of mixed cultures and races, of mixed political ideals and of differing religious followings. It can perhaps be argued that there is no public consensus on any moral issue. Cases in which the judiciary has had to consider differing moral positions include *Gillick* v *West Norfolk and Wisbech Area Health Authority* (1986), *Re A (Children)* (2000) and *ex parte Dianne Pretty* (2001).

Statements reflecting the pluralistic nature of society can be found in the Hart–Devlin debate. The Sexual Offences Act 1967 was introduced following recommendations made by the Wolfenden Committee in its 1957 report. The report prompted the debate. Professor Hart drew on the work of Professor John Stuart Mill who, in his essay 'On liberty', stated: '...the only part of the conduct of anyone, for which he is amenable to society, is that which concern others...Over himself, over his own body and mind, the individual is sovereign.' Hart and Mill believed it was immoral to make the minority conform to the will of the majority when in private. They recognised the pluralistic nature of society and the importance of individual liberty. Lord Devlin's views are more reflective of the late nineteenth-century criminal judge Sir James Stephen. Devlin believed that the loosening of moral bonds would lead to the disintegration of society. The law should punish acts which offend the common morality, whether done in public or in private.

Sir John Wolfenden followed the views of Mill and Hart. Their views were reflected in other reforming legislation of that decade including the Obscene Publications Act 1968 and the Divorce Law Reform Act 1969. The majority of the House of Lords in *Gillick* v *West Norfolk and Wisbech AHA* (1986) also adopted the Mill and Hart approach.

However, the influence of Stephen and Devlin can be seen in a number of judicial decisions. Perhaps the most significant recent decision is that of the House of Lords in *R* v *Brown & others* (1993) and the European Court of Human Rights in *Laskey, Brown & Jaggard* v *United Kingdom* (1997). The House of Lords held that the defence of consent could not be used in respect of sadomasochistic acts, which in this case were conducted in private. The European Court of Human Rights upheld the decision. Infringement of Article 8, the right to respect for private life, was justified by the need to protect health or morals.

The broad overlap of legal and moral rules is perhaps due to the characteristics they share. Both are concerned to impose certain standards of conduct without which it is difficult for society to exist, and both employ normative language. Laws, as Harris states, 'are found side by side with moral codes of greater or less complexity'.

There are, however, areas of divergence. There appears to be little moral justification for tobacco and alcohol consumption being legal and smoking of cannabis illegal. Similar arguments are raised by the legal requirement for pubs to close at 11 p.m. There are also moral rules which are not reinforced by legal rules. An example is the moral duty to help people who are in danger. The general position (there are exceptions) is that there is no legal liability for failing to act.

Natural law theorists would argue that legal rules which have no moral connection should not be afforded the status of law. According to Lloyd, the common thread running through the different views expressed as to what natural law is, is 'the constant assertion that there are objective moral principles which depend upon the nature of the universe'. Aristotle believed that the laws of nature constituted the natural law. St Thomas Aquinas believed that natural law was the divine law. In the mid-twentieth century, Professor Lon Fuller referred to the inner morality of law. To be valid the law had to conform to certain procedural requirements including consistency and being prospective.

In contrast, the positivists believe that whether a law is good or bad it is still valid. The origins of John Austin's command theory, whereby law is a command from a sovereign and enforced by a sanction, can be traced to Jeremy Bentham and Hobbes. Jeremy Bentham rejected natural law theories as 'nonsense on stilts'. Natural law was based on unprovable principles. What the law is, and what the law ought to be, should be treated as different issues.

Professor Hart also subscribes to the positivist view. From 1958 to 1967, a debate took place between Hart and Fuller. This was sparked by the views of the German philosopher Gustav Radbruch. According to Radbruch and Fuller, the Nazi laws which permitted atrocities should not have been regarded as valid. This was the view later adopted by the German courts. Hart, however, considered that the laws were legally valid but should have been challenged by people prepared to take the legal consequences.

In conclusion, it can be seen that there is a close relationship between legal and moral rules. A substantial body of English law is based on moral rules. The extent to which law should be influenced by morality remains topical. While it can be argued that a significant section of society has come to adopt the view taken by Professor Hart, there nevertheless remains a widely shared belief that weakening of the moral basis of law is dangerous.

> This is an outstanding answer, which approaches the theories in a sophisticated way. It is well-structured, comprehensive and yet concisely written. There is good use made of material drawn from many areas of the specification. The theories of the relationship between law and morality are soundly explained and illustrative material is used to demonstrate the influence of the theories on the development of the law. It would be awarded the maximum 30 marks.

■ ■ ■

C-grade answer

The laws in the UK are rules that apply to everyone, and if people break these rules they will be punished by the courts. An example of a punishment for breaking the law is the mandatory life sentence for murder. Another example of a punishment for breaking the law is a fine or ban from driving which people might get if they are caught speeding. Whether they get a fine or a ban will depend on how much they are speeding.

Morals are also rules. If people break moral rules, they will not be punished in the courts because they will not necessarily have broken the law. People who break moral rules, however, might get punished by friends and family who may not approve of their immoral behaviour.

A group of people called relativists believe that moral rules change over time and vary from place to place. Another group of people called realists believe that moral rules are, and have always been, the same and are eternally true or false.

Behaviour is sometimes both legally and morally wrong. For example, people think that rape and murder should be illegal, and the law agrees with this. If people rape or murder someone and get caught, then they will be given a serious punishment. If they are guilty of murder, they will definitely get a life sentence of 25 years. So with rape and murder the law and morals overlap. This is because the law reflects morals of society. This is also true with rape within marriage. Most people in society thought it was morally wrong for husbands to rape their wives and this was made illegal in *R v R*.

Theft is another example of an overlap of law and morals. Most people think it is morally wrong to steal something and there is a law on theft so that if people are caught stealing, they will be punished by the courts. They might get a fine or even go to prison depending on how much they have stolen. For example, if someone steals a car, he or she might get a harsher punishment than someone who steals a newspaper.

However, although law and morals sometimes overlap, there are times when they do not. Some laws have nothing to do with morals, such as what side of the road it is legal to drive on, and the law which requires pubs to shut at 11 p.m. In this country people are required to drive on the left-hand side of the road but in a lot of countries people are required to drive on the right-hand side of the road. Also in pubs, if the staff sell alcohol at 10.55 p.m. it is legal, but if they sell alcohol at 11.05 p.m. it is illegal.

Just as some laws have nothing to do with morals, some morals have nothing to do with law. Most people think it is immoral not to pay up if you have had a bet on something, for example a horse winning a race. However, if you place a bet on a horse and it wins and then the person who owes you your winnings does not pay you, the law will not make them pay you. Most people would agree too that it is not moral to cheat at sports, but the law will not punish you if you do. You might get punished by an organisation to do with the sport, but you will not be punished by the law.

There has been quite a lot of argument in recent years about what the connection between law and morality should be. This is sometimes referred to as the Hart–Devlin debate. The view of Professor Hart and his supporters is that the law should not interfere with what people do in private, while Lord Devlin argued that the law should regulate people's private behaviour. He believed that it was the law's role to uphold general standards of morality in order to prevent the disintegration of society.

This is a reasonable answer in that it is well structured and considers the characteristics of legal and moral rules and proceeds to discuss areas of coincidence and divergence. However, it is rather superficial in its approach. Furthermore, although realists and relativists are briefly referred to in connection with morals, little mention is made of the theories of the relationship between law and morality until the very end. It would be given 15 or 16 marks.

Law and justice

Consider the meaning of law and justice and the relationship between them. (30 marks)

■ ■ ■

A-grade answer

The law is a set of standardised procedures and mechanisms used in the enforcement of basic rights and the regulation of society. Sir John Salmond defined law as 'the principles used in the administration of justice'.

Justice is more difficult to define than law. Basically, it can be viewed as 'the principle of fairness', but this then leads to a discussion as to what 'fairness' means. This has led to many differing definitions of justice being put forward. There are two main ideas of justice — procedural and substantive.

Procedural justice views something as just if the correct procedures are followed, even if the procedures are not fair to begin with. Supporters of procedural justice say that for there to be justice it is important that everyone is treated in the same way and has the same rights. However, it is sometimes the case that it is not 'fair' for everyone to have the same rights. For example, the right to represent yourself is an important right, but is it appropriate in rape cases for the defendant to be able to cross-examine his alleged victim? This example shows that the law sometimes has to modify procedural justice in order to achieve real justice.

Another example of a difficulty arising in practice is the case of Dianne Pretty who was in the final stages of motor neurone disease and wanted her husband to help her die to avoid a distressing and undignified death. The European Court of Human Rights found against her and accepted the view that the ban on assisted suicides was just, and that to make an exception for Mrs Pretty would open the floodgates to other cases. Philip Havers in an article in *The Times* argued against the decision of the court on the basis that 'the ban on assisted suicides in England is indiscriminate, it catches everyone, not only the weak and vulnerable, who it is intended to protect, but also those like Mrs Pretty who neither need nor wish for the law's protection'. Furthermore, he argues that it is neither necessary nor proportionate to impose a blanket ban. In contrast Dr John Keown, arguing in favour of following consistent principles, quotes Dr Johnson who said that 'laws are not made for specific cases, but for men in general'.

Both these examples illustrate the connection between law and justice and the difficulty the law has with following procedural justice.

Substantive justice is the idea that something is just if it is inherently 'fair'. Attempts to define 'fair' have led to many differing definitions of justice.

Natural law theorists believe that there is a higher order of law and if this is followed, laws are just. If not, then not only is the law not just, but it cannot be considered a law at all and need not be obeyed. St Thomas Aquinas, for example, argued that law is God-given and therefore, if the laws based on Christian teaching are followed, the result will be justice. An unjust law might be contrary to human good or against the higher law derived from God. A law which went against this God-derived law would always be 'unjust' and should not be obeyed.

The Human Rights Act would suggest that there is a close connection between the law and the natural law theorists' concept of justice, because it incorporates into English law the European Convention on Human Rights which sets out 'fundamental' rights, such as freedom of expression and freedom from torture. Natural law theorists would support the decision in Dianne Pretty's case because it upholds the sanctity of human life.

An alternative theory is that of utilitarianism, argued by Jeremy Bentham, which measures the justice of a law on the basis of its consequences — if it benefits the majority, then it is just. This means that a law may create social inequalities, and benefit some at the expense of others, but if the gain to the majority exceeds the loss to the minority, then it is just.

Professor Rawls, in a view known as 'the original position', developed the idea of a just society being one which a group of rational but mutually disinterested people would unanimously choose to belong to if such a choice were available. He rejected the argument of utilitarianism and argued that inequality can only be just if that inequality is of benefit to all, not merely to the greatest number. He also argued that liberty must be respected and cannot be limited to promote greater happiness.

Utilitarians, and perhaps Professor Rawls, might argue that the law was applied unjustly in Mrs Pretty's case because she was disadvantaged and yet no one else benefited. Supporters of natural law, on the other hand, would argue that the sanctity of life is a fundamental principle, which cannot be compromised. It cannot be just to go against the 'higher law' and therefore the decision in Mrs Pretty's case was just.

The whole issue of euthanasia illustrates the problem of defining clearly the connection between law and justice. The law has somehow to find a path which represents a consensus, but this is difficult when there are different ideas about what is just in a particular situation. Is it just to uphold a fundamental principle like the sanctity of life or is it just to allow someone to choose death if they want to?

The connection between law and justice can be further examined by looking at the law on intoxication. In applying this defence the law makes a distinction between specific and basic level offences. This seems illogical because surely if you are too intoxicated to be capable of intention, then you are also incapable of subjective recklessness. Is it just to insist that for a person to be convicted of an offence, they must have *mens rea*, and yet to allow a person to be convicted when they are so intoxicated that they cannot form any *mens rea*? However, it would arguably not be just to allow this defence for all offences as this would mean that people who committed acts of violence when drunk would be perceived to be getting away with something for which a sober person would be convicted. There is also the issue of whether the victim would feel that justice had been done. One solution might be to deal with each case on its own merits and leave it to the common sense of the jury. But this in turn might raise the issue that defendants are not being treated equally, which would be against procedural justice.

In conclusion, it is clear that although some laws do not appear to be connected with ideas of justice, e.g. which side of the road we drive on, the law in general is closely connected with justice. Laws may become unenforceable if they go against prevailing views of what is just and it must be a fundamental principle of a democratic society that laws are based on ideas of justice. At the same time, it is clear that what may seem just to utilitarians might not appear just to supporters of natural law.

> This is a thoughtful and well-argued answer. It illustrates the fact that a very good answer can be written using a limited range of examples, providing that the examples are well chosen.
>
> The definition of law is rather brief, but the meaning of justice is explored fully and a number of theories are identified. The candidate has avoided the usual approach of writing a description of the theories followed by a series of examples of justice in practice. Instead, this answer genuinely tries to link ideas about justice with examples that illustrate them.
>
> The candidate also recognises that the question is about the connection between law and justice and this is frequently referred to and brought into the conclusion.
>
> The candidate has used material from other areas of the specification, but has also used examples, most notably that of Dianne Pretty, which have clearly been specifically prepared for this topic. The detailed quotes about this case are very effective.
>
> The candidate is not afraid to make personal observations, but they are appropriate and balanced by evidence from other sources.
>
> This answer would be awarded 26 or 27 marks out of 30.

■ ■ ■

C-grade answer

Laws are rules, which must be obeyed by everyone in society. They are rules made with authority and they are created and enforced by the state. Justice is about fairness — the idea that people should be treated in the same way. The legal system and legal rules should demonstrate that individuals are treated fairly and without bias.

There are many theories about justice. The Greek philosopher Aristotle, for example, identified two types of justice. Distributive justice is the allocation of assets, such as wealth and honour, in a proportionate way, not based on equal shares but instead on the contribution made by each individual. Corrective justice applies when distributive justice is interrupted by wrongdoing and involves punishing the offender and giving compensation to the victim.

Natural law theory is based on the idea that there is a higher order of law and if society follows this order, then it will be just. Some have argued that this law comes from nature, but St Thomas Aquinas said that it came from God. He argued that if a law conflicted with natural law, it need not be obeyed.

According to utilitarianism, put forward by J. S. Mill and Jeremy Bentham, society should work towards the greatest happiness for the greatest number, even if some individuals lose out. This means that as long as a law results in greater happiness for the majority, then it is just, even if it results in social inequality.

Karl Marx believed that it was impossible for a capitalist society to be just, as the laws are made to uphold the interests of the ruling class. Positivists like Kelsen believe that law is not related to morality or justice. They can contribute to the making of law, but law would still be law and would have to be obeyed even if it ignored ideas of justice — because these would only be expressions of personal preference, not fundamental truths.

There are examples of miscarriages of justice like the Bridgewater Four, who served many years in prison and one defendant actually died in prison, before it was proved that there were things wrong with the investigation. There were other miscarriages of justice as well, e.g. the Tottenham Three and the Birmingham Six.

Also, in criminal law the defence of provocation is not fair on women, because of the need for sudden and temporary loss of control. Any cooling off period would mean that the defence would fail. It is a fact that men are more likely to lose self-control than women. In cases like *Thornton*, where she killed her husband after suffering years of abuse, the defence failed because there was a cooling off period during which she went and sharpened a knife before attacking her husband. It has been argued that a woman could not just strike out like a man would because she would generally be physically weaker. Therefore this defence shows an injustice towards women.

The rules about the *mens rea* of murder are also a problem. Judges cannot look at motive, but only at whether there was intention. But if you compare a situation where someone helps a much-loved relative to die with one where someone deliberately kills as part of a robbery, it does not seem just that they are treated as equally blame-worthy and that both cases are treated as murder.

The fact of having juries creates injustice for some people, too. Although juries are picked at random, they can still have prejudices. In addition, as the Roskill Commission said, juries cannot understand complex fraud cases and may acquit someone wrongly, creating injustice for the victim. Jury nobbling with bribes or threats could also affect jury decisions and make them unfair.

question

So we can see that sometimes there is law without justice. This is important, not just because it is unfair to the individuals involved, but also because it leads people to have less respect for the law.

> ✏ This answer is clearly written in two halves. The theories of justice are well explained and appropriate examples of justice in practice are used, but the two are not really linked together. The examples are also rather briefly referred to and remain undeveloped.
>
> There is an attempt to relate law to justice and the practical examples illustrate this quite well, but there is little discussion of the relationship. The candidate needed to go on to say how the example illustrated the relationship.
>
> The conclusion is interesting because it does begin to discuss the implications of law without justice. These are the kind of points that should have been explored in depth earlier on in the essay.
>
> This answer would be worth 17 or 18 marks.

Balancing conflicting interests

How far can the law be used effectively to achieve a balance between conflicting interests?

(30 marks)

■ ■ ■

A-grade answer

In every area of law there are potentially conflicting interests. An important reason for having law is to set out rules, which should apply and ensure that all relevant interests are considered and possible conflicts averted. For example, the rules on the making of contracts or the rules on intestacy are designed to ensure that people know what they have to do to ensure that their interests are protected.

The law also has to provide machinery — courts and tribunals — which ensure that if conflicts of interest do occur there is a means of settling them in a way which tries to balance the opposing views as fairly as possible.

In the nineteenth century, von Jhering suggested that society needed law to regulate the conflicts that would inevitably arise between the many different interests and argued that law acted as a mediator between these various competing interests. The American academic Roscoe Pound suggested that there are two types of interests — individual interests, such as owning property, and social interests, i.e. those that affect everyone collectively. He also suggested that you can only balance individual interests against other individual interests and social interests against other social interests.

By interests we mean rights or desires which a person or group might have. In some situations, e.g. a simple contract, there may just be two parties, both of whom have rights because they are both bringing something of value to the agreement. In other situations there may be a variety of interests of different kinds, e.g. when a paedophile is being sentenced.

In some situations the law may have to favour one side in order to redress what is an unequal balance, e.g. the statutory rules relating to implied terms and exclusion clauses.

In practice, the courts do not follow Roscoe Pound's idea that you can only balance interests of the same kind, and one way of considering how effectively the law is able to balance interests is to compare public interests and private interests. On the whole, it could be argued that where public and private interests are in conflict it is the public interest that will prevail.

For example, in private nuisance the law is concerned to achieve a balance between an occupier's quiet enjoyment of his or her land and a neighbour's legitimate use of his or her land. In *Miller* v *Jackson*, the conflict involved an application for an injunction against a cricket club by residents whose properties adjoined the cricket ground. Lord Denning approached the problem in terms of 'a conflict between the interests of the public at large and the interests of a private individual'. Denning concluded that the public interest outweighed the individual one and refused to grant the injunction, although he did attempt to balance this by awarding damages to compensate for the inconvenience of having cricket balls regularly hit into your garden. This issue could have been approached in terms of one individual's private interest in enjoying his garden against the private interest of a group of people in playing cricket, but often the public interest is much more obvious, and involves an activity that benefits the community at large at the expense of a few individuals. In these cases there will often be statutory support for the activity. Railways, airports and motorways will all interfere with the enjoyment of land, but private interests will not be allowed to obstruct the public interest.

A recent example is the case of *Marcic* v *Thames Water* in which the claimant's house was regularly flooded with sewage. The House of Lords confirmed that the Water Industry Act 1991 excluded a remedy in nuisance. The balance here was clearly in favour of the public interest (the Water Companies), which would not be served if householders could demand expensive modifications to water treatment plants. On the other hand, the courts may be willing to award compensation where private interests have been damaged by public interests. In one unreported case in 2003, a householder was awarded almost a £1m compensation for disturbance caused by military aircraft from a nearby airbase.

Another obvious area of conflict between public and private interests is the protection of human rights, and the passing of the Human Rights Act 1998 would seem to emphasise the private over the public interest. However, often the relevant articles of the European Convention on Human Rights have derogation clauses specifically to allow the public interest to take precedence. For example, under Article 8 everyone has the right to respect for his private and family life, his home and his correspondence. It also expressly provides that this can be overridden in the interests of things like national security, public safety, the economic well-being of the country or the protection of health or morals. In *Marcic* v *Thames Water*, mentioned earlier, an attempt to use Article 8 was rejected by the House of Lords.

Another area in which we can see interests being balanced is consumer protection law. Here the role of the law historically was to establish rules to enable people to enforce contracts that they had freely entered into. Freedom of contract meant that the courts were reluctant to interfere with what the parties had agreed. But the resources and bargaining position of the parties in consumer transactions were clearly not equal and therefore the law, largely through statutory regulations, has intervened to protect the weaker party — the consumer. It is only in recent years that the consumer has been identified as someone with different interests to other contractual parties, most notably in legislation like the Unfair Contract Terms Act 1977, which does much to redress the imbalance created by the use of exclusion clauses, and the

Consumer Protection Act 1987, which establishes what is in effect strict liability in respect of defective goods which injure people.

The need for balance can also be seen in criminal law. We can see the public interest in the need to ensure public order and protect the lives and property of citizens. Against this can be placed the private interests of individual defendants to have a fair trial and the private needs of victims who will want what they perceive to be 'justice' in the case. When we look at the whole range of provisions, we can see that the law is trying to achieve balance — certain activities are declared either through statutes or case law to be unlawful, and appropriate punishments are imposed to protect the public. At the same time, rules of evidence and the burden of proof protect the defendant, while victims are able to claim compensation from the Criminal Injuries Compensation Board, even if no one is convicted.

But the frequent changes to the rules by successive governments and almost constant discussion of law and order in the press and by politicians suggest that the balance in this area is far from effective. The previous (Conservative) government introduced the unit fine system (matching the size of fine with offenders' incomes) in the Criminal Justice Act 1991 which was widely criticised because, although it tried to achieve balance by making fines more equal in their effect, it was seen as unfair. Equally, the Crime Sentencing Act 1997, which introduced mandatory sentences in an attempt to protect the public, was criticised by judges as preventing them from being fair to individual offenders. The present government has made a number of changes to the criminal justice system in an attempt to achieve a more effective balance. For example, it has modified the right to silence and allowed the seizure of drug dealers' assets. It has also tried to restrict the right to jury trial. Specific measures to deal with the threat of terrorism have been even more draconian and, at the time of writing, the House of Lords is deliberating on whether the legislation allowing the detention without trial of suspected terrorists is lawful.

The problem is, of course, that the issues raised by these measures are hugely important. On the one hand, there is a danger that governments will use the excuse of crime or terrorism to increase the power of the state, while on the other hand, the private interests of the overwhelming majority of citizens as well as the public interest demand much tougher measures.

In conclusion, it is evident that achieving balance is not easy. In some areas, e.g. consumer rights, it could be argued that the law has been effective in achieving balance, but in many areas, particularly those where public interests are in conflict with private interests, the law has been much less successful in achieving a successful balance.

> This is an excellent answer, which would be awarded 29 or 30 marks. It is well structured and proceeds in a logical, systematic way. The candidate begins by considering generally how the law is there to balance interests, and never loses sight of the fact that this is what the question is about. A wide range of examples

is used, from many areas of law, but they are always linked to the theme of balancing interests.

Reference is made to theories and they are also related to the examples. The relationship between public and private interests is particularly well explored.

The answer also addresses the issue of effectiveness and the essay is rounded off with a clear and thoughtful conclusion.

The only weakness is that it is rather long. Examiners often see one excellent answer and one much shorter one, indicating that the student has run out of time.

■ ■ ■

C-grade answer

The law has to balance many different interests and settle conflicts. The writer Roscoe Pound said that there were different kinds of interests — public and private — and that each could only be balanced against other interests of the same kind.

There are many areas of law where we can see interests being balanced. In criminal law, the interests of the defendant have to be balanced against the interests of the victim and the state. These interests are obviously in conflict. The law helps victims by taking over all the investigation of crimes and the prosecution. Victims are also paid compensation for injuries they receive as a result of a crime. The law has to protect the public generally, so the police are given powers to take such measures as stopping and searching suspects, although this is restricted under the Police and Criminal Evidence Act (1984) (PACE). They can also arrest people for serious offences and question them, and carry out raids with search warrants.

But defendants are also protected. The police have to carry out procedures according to the rules, e.g. caution people when arresting them, and they can only question people for a certain length of time before either charging them or releasing them. Defendants have advantages in court too. The burden of proof is on the prosecution and guilt must be proved beyond reasonable doubt. There are restrictions on evidence that can be used, e.g. uncorroborated confessions, and the defence has to see all the prosecution evidence in order to prepare its case properly.

There is a balance in the way actual crimes work, because people can only be found guilty if there is *actus reus* and *mens rea*. For example, in murder you need to prove that the defendant caused death — both factual causation, i.e. the 'but for' rule, and legal causation (must be a significant cause). You also need to prove either intent to cause GBH (Cunningham/Vickers) or intent to kill. There is also oblique intent, which is where the jury is satisfied that the defendant knew that death or serious injury was virtually certain.

Defences to crimes also help to achieve balance. Provocation is a defence only to murder, but it means that if defendants can prove that they were provoked, they will be guilty of manslaughter. You have to prove provocative conduct (e.g. *Doughty*), sudden and temporary loss of control and that the 'reasonable' person would have behaved in the same way. Some women's groups have argued that this defence is not fair to women and cases such as *Thornton* and *Ahluwahlia* show that if you have a delay before you kill, you cannot use the defence of provocation.

Civil law is also about achieving balance. For example, the rules of nuisance try to balance the interests of people occupying land with those of their neighbours. A case like *Miller* v *Jackson* is a good example. The law had to balance the right of people to enjoy their gardens in safety against the wish of others to play cricket. In *Rylands* v *Fletcher* the decision was that you would be liable if you brought something onto your land for a non-natural use, which would cause mischief if it escaped. Water from Fletcher's reservoir flooded mines belonging to Rylands. In occupiers' liability there is also balance because the occupier owes a different duty to lawful visitors and trespassers.

In the area of law and morality, the law can sometimes seem to be unfair. For example, in *Brown* the court decided that sadomasochism was not lawful, even though all the men consented, whereas in *Wilson* it was lawful for a man to cut his initials into his wife's buttocks.

One case which illustrates conflicting interests is *Re A (Children)* (2000). In this case, if an operation were carried out to separate Siamese twins, then one of them would die. The hospital wanted to operate because otherwise both would die, but the parents did not want the operation to take place. The court listened to the arguments of the doctors and decided in their favour. This suggests that the law can be effective in achieving balance between conflicting interests.

It can be seen that in most areas of law there are interests to balance. The job of the courts is to do this. Judges have a great deal of responsibility for balancing the law. One of the problems is that they might be biased. They have been criticised for their political bias, e.g. in the GCHQ case, and some people say that it is not fair that judges choose which rule they want to use when they interpret statutes. In addition, is it right that the Lord Chancellor, and even the prime minister, has so much influence in choosing judges?

So there are problems with the law balancing interests, but in some areas it is quite effective.

> 🖉 This answer covers a range of relevant areas and attempts to deal with the issue of balance. There is very little theoretical material, and although Roscoe Pound is mentioned, his ideas are not related to the rest of the answer. There is no attempt to consider the different types of interest in the examples chosen.
>
> The section on the rights of victims and defendants is good, and the way in which the law tries to balance the different interests is well explained, but the section on murder is largely descriptive. An opportunity to talk about how effectively the law

achieves balance is offered by the comments on women and provocation, but the answer fails to pursue this.

At several points the examples could have been related more closely with what the question is asking, but only once does the answer talk about effectiveness — when discussing *Re A (Children)* (2000). The analysis here is brief and limited.

This answer had a lot of promise but it is undeveloped. All the examples are potentially relevant, and they could have been used to develop discussion about how successful the law is in achieving balance. It would be awarded 17 or 18 marks.

Fault

Discuss how far fault is an essential requirement for liability in English law, and consider whether fault should be an essential requirement.

(30 marks)

■ ■ ■

A-grade answer

Both the *Concise Oxford Dictionary* and the *Collins Concise Dictionary* define fault in terms of 'responsibility' and 'culpability' or 'blame' for something wrong. Responsibility is defined by both dictionaries in terms of ability to take rational decisions, and rational is defined by both dictionaries in terms of reasonableness. Perhaps the core meaning of fault to emerge through these definitions is 'responsibility for something wrong', although the other definitions will also feature in the ensuing discussion.

Fault is generally an essential requirement of liability in the law of tort. Liability in negligence requires proof of a breach of duty. A breach of duty arises when the defendant fails to act, or not act, as the 'reasonable man' would have done. In *Bolton* v *Stone* (1951), the defendants acted as the 'reasonable man' would have by erecting a high fence around the ground to minimise the risk of people outside the ground being injured by cricket balls. In *Paris* v *Stepney Borough Council* (1951), however, the court held that, in light of the potential serious consequences posed by welding to an employee with one eye, the reasonable employer would have provided goggles. Liability under the Occupiers' Liability Act 1957 also requires proof of fault. Under s.2 (2) (b) a lower duty of care is owed to people on the premises in exercise of their calling, than to other visitors. In *Roles* v *Nathan* (1963), the occupiers were not liable when chimney sweeps died from inhaling fumes. They had warned the sweeps of the risk, and it was the responsibility of the sweeps to be aware of the danger.

Fault is also relevant to the general defence of contributory negligence. Under the Law Reform (Contributory Negligence) Act 1945 s.1(1), damages are reduced according to the claimant's responsibility for the damage. In *Froom* v *Butcher* (1975), the claimant's damages were reduced by 25% due to his failure to wear a seat belt.

There are, however, areas of tort in which there is no need to prove fault. For example, nuisance is a strict liability tort. The defendant cannot claim as a defence that he/she took reasonable care to avoid causing the nuisance. The rule in *Rylands* v *Fletcher* is another strict liability tort. However, since the case of *Cambridge Water Company* v *Eastern Counties Leather plc* (1994), negligence principles have applied in respect of the type of damage caused having to be foreseeable.

It is important also to consider the principle of vicarious liability, which imposes liability for someone else's fault. In the workplace, the employer is liable for torts committed by employees during the course of their employment. This includes torts committed while the employee is doing what he/she is authorised to do but doing it in an unauthorised manner. In *Rose* v *Plenty* (1976), the employer had expressly forbidden employees to allow people to ride on the milk floats. The employer was, nevertheless, vicariously liable, when a 13-year-old boy was injured while helping an employee deliver milk.

So far, we have considered how fault is generally a requirement for liability in tort, albeit that there are some exceptions. There is also a general principle of no liability without proof of fault in criminal law.

To be found guilty of most criminal offences an *actus reus* and *mens rea* must be present. The *actus reus* must usually be committed voluntarily. If the accused is not in control of his/her actions, there are general defences that the accused may raise, including insanity, automatism and duress. In *R* v *Bailey* (1983), the accused, a diabetic, successfully pleaded the defence of automatism. He had been in a hypoglycaemic state brought about by a failure to eat after drinking some sugar and water.

The *mens rea* comprises the mental element of the crime. All of the non-fatal offences except that provided by s.18 of the Offences Against the Person Act 1861 are crimes of basic intent. Section 18 is a specific intent crime. All the non-fatal offences, therefore, require proof of fault for a conviction. Similarly, all homicide offences require proof of fault. Murder is the most serious homicide offence. The accused must intend to kill or cause grievous bodily harm. The seriousness of the offence is recognised in the mandatory sentence of life imprisonment.

While fault is an essential requirement of liability in most crimes, there are nevertheless some strict liability and some absolute liability offences. Strict liability crimes have no fault requirement in terms of *mens rea*. In *Smedleys* v *Breed* (1974), the defendants were convicted despite having taken all reasonable precautions to prevent contamination of their food products occurring. Absolute liability crimes, however, have no fault requirement either in respect of the *mens rea* or the *actus reus*. In *Winzar* v *Chief Constable of Kent* (1983), the accused was convicted of being found drunk on the highway after he had been forcefully removed from a hospital and placed on the highway by the police.

The injustice of the decision in *Winzar* is clear. The defendant did not voluntarily commit the offence and arguably should not therefore have had to bear legal responsibility for it. There are very few absolute liability offences, so convictions such as this are rare. However, there are numerous strict liability offences. Strict liability offences are usually justified on the basis that they are for the public good, and they typically deal with issues such as public health and safety, protection of the environment and road traffic. There is the further advantage that court time is saved and costs are reduced when there is no need to prove *mens rea*. Those in favour of strict liability offences argue also that a higher standard of care is encouraged. However, there is no concrete evidence of this.

The legal profession, the judges and the legislature regard the principle of no liability without proof of fault as being especially important in criminal law. A guilty verdict will result in the imposition of a sentence on the defendant and in addition, arguably more importantly, a criminal record. The court has a wide range of sentences, 'at its disposal, some of which directly limit the liberty of the convict, including electronic tagging, probation and incarceration. However, the liberty of the convicted individual is also affected by his/her criminal record, which may, for example, prevent access to certain jobs. The imposition of state sanctions and the restriction of liberty are generally regarded as justified only when the individual has been responsible for his/her actions.

The civil law is also based on the notion of individual responsibility. Individuals choose to behave the way they do and should therefore accept responsibility for the outcomes of their actions. However, while liability in civil law is generally based on proof of fault, there has been a shift towards no-fault liability in recent years.

Legislation of the twentieth century now provides a partial no-fault based system. This is because the requirement to prove fault results in most accident victims not receiving any compensation. The Welfare State legislation created the Department of Social Security. Victims of accidents at work are now able to claim compensation from the state, without the need to prove negligence. Social security benefits are also available to those who suffer illness or disability. While such legislation provides compensation for more accident victims, it clearly penalises all members of society who have to pay for the actions of a blameworthy few. Since the enactment of the Consumer Protection Act 1987, producers have been strictly liable for damage caused by their defective products. However, although the producer directly provides the compensation to the claimant, the burden is indirectly borne by society. Producers inevitably recoup the money by raising the prices of their goods.

There are, however, many accident victims who are required to prove fault, including road accident victims and victims of medical negligence. It is argued that the cost of insurance would have to rise to unaffordable levels were no-fault based liability to be imposed.

In conclusion, it would appear that fault should be a requirement of liability more so in criminal law than in civil law. The unfairness of leaving an injured victim without compensation increasingly outweighs the unfairness of blameless individuals being required to provide compensation out of state funds. In criminal law, however, the desire to protect the blameless individual from the outcomes of a criminal conviction makes imposition of liability without fault less acceptable.

> ✓ This is a comprehensive, well-structured answer. Both aspects of the question, 'is' and 'should', are considered extensively and accurately. Excellent use is made of illustrative material throughout. This answer would be awarded 29 or 30 marks.

C-grade answer

In English law there is a general requirement that liability depends on the proof of fault. This can be seen in the law of tort and crime. Although generally proof of fault is a just requirement, there are situations where it does not lead to a just outcome.

Fault is an essential requirement in negligence and occupiers' liability. In negligence, three elements must be proved for an action to succeed: first, it must be proved that the defendant owed a duty of care; second it must be proved that the defendant breached this duty; and, finally, it must be proved that the plaintiff suffered some form of harm as a result of such a breach. To establish whether the defendant was at fault, the courts will apply the standard of the 'reasonable man'. This is done by taking into account the likelihood of the incident happening, the cost of removing such a risk and the seriousness of the incident. This is shown in *Bolton* v *Stone* (1951), when the plaintiff was hit by a cricket ball which had cleared a 17-foot fence. It was held that the defendant had done what was considered reasonable to stop this by putting up such a high fence. He was therefore not at fault.

Fault also has to be proved in occupiers' liability. It is stated in the Occupiers' Liability Act 1957 that the occupier owes the visitor the common duty of care. It also states that professionals are owed less of a duty of care as they are supposed to know what they are doing on the premises. Children are owed a higher duty of care because they cannot look after themselves as well as adults.

In some areas of tort, liability does not depend on proving fault. Unlike in negligence and occupiers' liability, nuisance does not depend on fault, as it is a strict liability tort. But if the defendant is malicious, this will be taken into consideration.

Rylands v *Fletcher* is also a strict liability tort. The defendant is liable if he uses his land for a non-natural use, or if something on his land escapes and causes damage. There is no need to prove negligence.

Vicarious liability is another area where there is no need to prove fault. The defendant is liable for someone else's wrongdoing. This usually happens in the workplace, when employers are liable to compensate people who have been harmed by their workers.

The principle of no liability without fault is also important in the criminal law. Most crimes consist of an *actus reus* and a *mens rea*. The *mens rea* reflects the mental state of the defendant when he/she commits a crime. For the law on homicide, a mental element is required. The offences contained within the Offences Against the Person Act (1861) also require a certain level of fault. Assault and battery, sections 47 and 20, both require intention or recklessness. However, the offence of GBH with intent under s.18 requires intention to be proved. It is not enough for a conviction if the accused is only reckless.

In these aspects of criminal law, that is homicide and non-fatal offences, liability depends on fault being proved, but strict liability offences also exist. Strict liability offences do not require proof of *mens rea* and the prosecution only has to prove the *actus reus*. Examples of these sorts of offences are traffic offences like parking on a yellow line or speeding. As long as it can be proved that the accused was speeding or on a yellow line, he/she will be found guilty. The court will not be concerned with his/her state of mind while he/she was speeding or parking on the yellow line.

There are advantages of requiring fault, the most obvious one being that it means that the law punishes people who are blameworthy. However, there are also disadvantages. There are a lot of people who suffer injury caused by the negligence of others who end up with no compensation because it is sometimes hard to prove fault.

In conclusion, it can be seen that most of English law does depend on proof of fault, although there are some laws which do not depend on it. Liability should depend on fault because only the blameworthy should be punished.

This question clearly has two parts. Candidates are required to consider how far fault *is* a requirement of liability **and** to what extent fault *should be* a requirement of liability. In addressing these issues, candidates are expected to provide illustrative material drawn from the specification.

Overall, this is a reasonable answer. The answer includes consideration of how far fault is a requirement of liability in the law of tort through a discussion of negligence, occupiers' liability, nuisance, *Rylands* v *Fletcher* and the principle of vicarious liability. The breadth of law referred to is commendable. However, for a higher grade, the answer should include more reference to authority, and more explanation of the fault/no fault elements of each tort. While the answer indicates some understanding of the role of fault in criminal law, the material used is somewhat superficial. The part of the answer considering to what extent fault should be a requirement of liability is very brief. The answer merely gives one advantage and one disadvantage of the requirement to prove fault. This is a common weakness in answers given by candidates to the fault question.

Overall this answer would be awarded **16 or 17 marks**.

Question 5

Judicial creativity

Referring to precedent and statutory interpretation, discuss how creative judges can be, and compare the contributions made by the judiciary and Parliament to the development of the law. (30 marks)

■ ■ ■

A-grade answer

The constitutional role of the judiciary is to apply the law that Parliament makes. However, judges have the power to change rules or make new rules through precedent or statutory interpretation.

The doctrine of precedent is based on the requirement that judges must follow decisions made in earlier cases, and on the face of it would seem to limit their freedom to be creative. First of all, there is the hierarchy of the courts, which means that courts are bound by decisions of other courts higher up in the hierarchy. Under the 1966 Practice Direction, the House of Lords is allowed to depart from its own earlier decisions, as for example in *Hetherington* v *British Rail* and *R* v *Shivpuri*, but the Court of Appeal is bound by its own earlier decisions, despite Lord Denning's efforts. The binding part of the judgement is called the *ratio decidendi* and later courts are bound to follow the legal principles on which the decision was based if their case contains similar facts. *Obita dicta* — other things said not directly related to the decision or dissenting judgements — are persuasive rather than binding precedents. The system of precedent requires detailed and accurate law reports.

In fact, judges are able to exercise considerable creativity, despite the constraints of precedent. In some areas of law, like contract law, negligence and fatal offences, judges make nearly all the legal rules. An example of a very creative judgement was *Donoghue* v *Stevenson*, which established the modern law of negligence. Another good example is *R* v *R*, which introduced the idea that a husband could be guilty of rape if he forced his wife to have sex.

The House of Lords can use the Practice Direction and so, in theory, has almost unlimited power to change earlier precedents. In fact, it uses this power with restraint, but on several occasions it has exercised creativity and altered the law. In the recent case of *R* v *G* it overturned *R* v *Caldwell* and decided that recklessness must always be subjective.

There are also other ways that courts can be creative. Sometimes there is no precedent and judges can use legal reasoning, persuasive precedents, argue from analogy etc. as in *Hunter* v *Canary Wharf*. Judges can also distinguish the case from the precedent by arguing that the facts are materially different. *Merritt* v *Merritt* did not follow the earlier case of *Balfour* v *Balfour* because although both cases concerned agreements between husbands and wives, in the latter case they were separated. Higher courts can, of course, reverse decisions of lower courts, as in *Gillick* and *Tomlinson* v *Congleton BC* (the recent occupiers' liability case), where the House of Lords reversed Court of Appeal decisions, and it can overrule earlier precedents by lower courts.

When interpreting statutes, courts have less opportunity to be creative. Their powers are largely limited to explaining ambiguous or unclear wording, though sometimes they are asked to rule on wording which is clear but seems to go against common sense or the spirit of the Act. In all these situations they have aids to help them, which allow some creativity. For example, they can refer to other parts of the Act or to a report, e.g. by the Law Commission on which the Act was based. Following the decision in *Pepper* v *Hart*, they can also refer to ministerial statements in Parliament in certain limited circumstances.

What is much more controversial is whether judges should be able to change the wording of a statute to arrive at what it is presumed Parliament intended to say. Supporters of the literal rule, such as Viscount Simmonds, say that to do this would be to usurp the role of Parliament and therefore be wrong. But creative judges like Lord Denning argued that it was the duty of the court to fill in the gaps and look for what Parliament intended to say. When judges use the mischief rule/purposive approach, they are in effect prepared to change the literal and often clear meaning of words in order to arrive at what Parliament intended. For example, in *Royal College of Nursing* v *DHSS*, the Abortion Act case, they changed 'by a registered medical practitioner' to 'under the supervision of ...'.

Judges who follow the literal rule will be less creative. They prefer the security of preserving the status quo and offer as justification their respect of parliamentary sovereignty. *Fisher* v *Bell* is a good example. It was clear under contract law that a knife in a shop window was not being 'offered' for sale, and therefore applying the literal rule the defendant was not guilty. Parliament had created this situation through its wording in the Act and Parliament would have to change it.

Judges can use the 'golden rule', where the wording creates an absurd or repugnant situation as in *Sigsworth* (where, if taken literally, the Act would allow a man to inherit from his mother, whom he had murdered) or *Adler* v *George*.

It seems that in more recent times judges are being encouraged to use the purposive approach and thus be more creative. This is partly because of the influence of the European Union law, which is drafted in general terms and assumes judges will fill in the detail. Also of great importance is the Human Rights Act, which allows judges to consider whether an Act complies with the European Convention on Human Rights.

When comparing the roles of Parliament and judges, it is obvious that there is a place for both in law making. In many areas of law, Parliament has chosen not to become involved and increasingly it has less time for law reform. There is nothing anti-democratic in judges making new principles of law, as long as Parliament has the right ultimately to overrule the decision.

Parliament is able to be much more creative than judges for several reasons. First, unlike judges, it can choose the time to legislate. Judges have to wait for a suitable case to be brought. In addition, judges can only consider evidence presented by the parties in the case. They cannot consider arguments about the general social or economic or moral aspects, even though their decision, e.g. in *Gillick*, may have implications for society generally. When Parliament legislates, the views of all interested people or groups are actively sought.

Judges can only make law on the facts before them and cannot, unlike Parliament, set out a code of rules to cover all similar situations. It does not help when one small change is made, e.g. the reintroduction of gross negligence manslaughter in *Prentice/Adomako*, when really the whole area needs to be properly reformed. Judge-made law operates retrospectively, too, which is why the House of Lords would not accept Denning's idea of the matrimonial car in *Morgans* v *Launchbury*.

Another problem is that changing the law frequently creates uncertainty and this explains why the House of Lords is reluctant to use the Practice Direction (e.g. in *Knuller* it would not overrule Shaw).

In conclusion it can be seen that judges can be creative, but that they are, and should be, less creative than Parliament. It is also evident that judges are playing a more significant creative role because of the UK's membership of the European Union and because of the Human Rights Act.

This is a full answer, packed with relevant examples from several parts of the specification.

The question asks you to cover a lot of material. It requires some reference to precedent and statutory interpretation and how the rules affect the ability of judges to be creative. It then requires a comparison with the way Parliament works. This answer deals with all these aspects and is clearly structured and systematic.

One of its strengths is that it never becomes a purely descriptive answer. It frequently refers back to the question and makes appropriate analytical comment.

It is a balanced and clear answer and would be awarded 29 or 30 marks.

■ ■ ■

C-grade answer

The development of law by Parliament takes a long time and so is supported by judicial creativity and the ability of judges to change and develop some points of law.

The doctrine of precedent allows judges to intervene in the law, although there is still some control on them through binding and persuasive precedent. The hierarchy of the court structure means that all courts, except the House of Lords, are bound by higher courts and those of equal status. The House of Lords can use the Practice Direction, which allows it to overturn existing precedents, e.g. *British Rail* v *Herrington*. By being allowed to do this, there is definite opportunity for judicial creativity.

The concept of precedent can be described in the phrase '*stare decisis*' or 'to stand by things decided'. It appears in the form of comments made by the judge, either *ratio decidendi* or *obiter dicta*. *Ratio decidendi* is a binding precedent, but *obiter dicta* means comments made along the way. For example, in deciding that duress is not a valid defence to murder, it was said *obiter* that it would not be available for attempted murder either.

The power that judges have to make law is effective and does not need to be referred to Parliament. Whole areas of law, such as the law on murder or negligence, are made by judges, without the involvement of Parliament. For example, the law on the *mens rea* of murder developed through cases like *Hyam*, *Moloney*, *Hancock* and *Shankland* and finally *Nedrick* and *Woollin*.

Statutory interpretation is another way in which judges make law. Sometimes it is necessary for judges to consider other information if a statute is unclear or not sufficiently precise. Judges are allowed to refer to *Hansard* and to dictionaries and other statutes in an attempt to discover exactly what Parliament intended. There are a range of opinions on the extent to which judges should interpret statutes. Some believe that the exact wording should be followed at all times, for example in *Berriman*. In this case, a railway worker had been killed while oiling points. The widow claimed compensation, but the Act said that she would only be eligible if he had been killed whilst repairing the line. As Berriman had only been oiling the points, he was not repairing and therefore the widow could not claim.

Some judges prefer to use the mischief rule or purposive approach. For example, in *Smith* v *Hughes*, a prostitute was seen to be tapping on her window in order to attract the attention of men passing in the street. Even though the Act required her to be soliciting in a street and she was in her flat, the mischief that the Act sought to counter was prostitutes harassing people who were in the street, so therefore she was guilty.

Judges can also use the 'golden rule' to prevent a morally repugnant outcome, as demonstrated in *Sigsworth*. A son had murdered his mother but under the relevant Act he would inherit her property under the intestacy rules. The court decided that this would be ludicrous and so the wording of the Act was changed.

If judges were not able to be flexible in using these rules, there would be many more injustices. In the majority of cases, though, precedents are followed and the literal rule is used in statutory interpretation, so that judges are making a fairly small contribution to law making, compared with Parliament.

🔁 This is a much more limited answer. It covers the rules on precedent and statutory interpretation reasonably well, though the section on statutory interpretation in particular is largely descriptive, with no reference to how this material is related to creativity.

There are comments about creativity and the points about the Practice Direction and the *mens rea* of murder are good. However, these are isolated points and the evaluative comments are brief.

Both the opening and the closing sentences refer to the comparison with Parliament and suggest that the student has an understanding of the issues. However, these points are generalised and not taken further.

This is an outline answer that makes reference to all the relevant areas, but remains undeveloped, with relatively little evaluation. It would score 17 or 18 marks.